Money for Content and Your Clicks for Free: Turning Web Sites, Blogs, and Podcasts Into Cash

JD Frazer

WILEY

Wiley Publishing, Inc.

Money for Content and Your Clicks for Free: Turning Web Sites, Blogs, and Podcasts Into Cash

Published by
Wiley Publishing, Inc.
10475 Crosspoint Boulevard
Indianapolis, IN 46256
www.wiley.com

Published simultaneously in Canada

ISBN-13: 978-0-471-74753-6
ISBN-10: 0-471-74753-X

Manufactured in the United States of America

10 9 8 7 6 5 4 3 2 1

1MA/QR/RR/QV/IN

For general information on our other products and services or to obtain technical support, please contact our Customer Care Department within the U.S. at (800) 762-2974, outside the U.S. at (317) 572-3993 or fax (317) 572-4002.

Wiley also publishes its books in a variety of electronic formats. Some content that appears in print may not be available in electronic books.

Library of Congress Cataloging-in-Publication Data is available from the publisher.

About the Author

JD Frazer (BC, Canada) is a cartoonist and writer who enjoys a readership in excess of 1.5 million fans internationally. His site, `Userfriendly.org`, is the first stop on the Web in the morning for a vast number of Information Technology professionals. He has spoken at more than 50 events as both keynote speaker and panelist, on topics related to the business of online content, intellectual property, and online communities. He has consulted for companies on online consumer trends, online community development, and content development. His popular books with O'Reilly and Associates have sold more than 100,000 copies.

Credits

Executive Editor
Chris Webb

Development Editor
Kevin Shafer

Technical Editor
Ken Fisher

Production Editor
Angela Smith

Copy Editor
Kim Cofer

Editorial Manager
Mary Beth Wakefield

Production Manager
Tim Tate

Vice President & Executive Group Publisher
Richard Swadley

Vice President and Publisher
Joseph B. Wikert

Project Coordinator
Ryan Steffen

Graphics and Production Specialists
Lauren Goddard
Denny Hager
Stephanie D. Jumper
Barbara Moore
Lynsey Osborn
Heather Ryan

Quality Control Technician
Laura Albert

Proofreading and Indexing
TECHBOOKS Production Services

This one is for Gret

All guys should be so lucky.

Preface

Immature poets imitate; mature poets steal.

— *Thomas Stearns Eliot, 1888–1965*

What you hold in your hands is a window of sorts, the kind of window with which you watch a particular world go by. This book is about the burgeoning business of making money—and perhaps a living—as a content provider on the World Wide Web. That particular world hasn't had much exposure since its birth largely because even the Big Companies are new to the game. Making money from putting up digital work was, for quite some time, unthinkable to many, and hard to accept for the rest. But everything matures, if it lives long enough, and despite the bottom dropping out during the Dot Bomb years ago, the independent creator on the Web has prevailed and remained. Getting to this point was certainly not bloodless; thankfully it was also highly educational.

This book is about so many things regarding the online content business that it might be easier for me to list what it isn't:

- It's not a manual that explains how to use Photoshop, InDesign, or your favorite blogging tool.

- It doesn't tell you how to create podcasts.

- It doesn't explain how to lay down a backbeat track for your latest techno composition.

- It doesn't cover the use of Dreamweaver, nor does it tell you what makes for good Web design and what doesn't.

In other words, it doesn't tell you how to make digital content. That skill, talent, and drive I assume you already have, or you probably wouldn't be reading this book.

This book also doesn't explain the technical aspects of delivering content on the Web. Explanations of HTTP requests and TCP/IP belong in books about networking. Also, I assume that you know how to use a Web browser, an FTP client, or whatever it is that you need to get your content out to the Net At Large. If you have no idea how to do this, I recommend you talk to a friend who does (or perhaps a friend's child), because this is outside the scope of the book.

If you're looking to run your own business, there is some fundamental knowledge you need to have regardless of the nature of that business. I assume you know how to obtain a business license, keep records of accounts using generally accepted accounting principles, incorporate a business, and all of the other "administrivia" that comes with starting up a small concern. Much of these requirements vary from locale to locale, so covering them here would be pointless.

What I present to you in this book is business perspective. After being in this particular game for close to a decade, I've had (and unfortunately took) the opportunity to make every pertinent mistake imaginable. But I've learned from those mistakes and hope that I can help you sidestep them in your own quest to be paid for the content you create and share with others. I've been a full-time independent creator since 1997, and, as such, most of what I've written in this book will be from the vantage point of someone who relies on the Web to put food on the table. This isn't to say that this book isn't meant for those of you who are only looking for a little beer money. Most of everything I teach in this book can be applied directly to a part-time content effort with no modification at all. On occasion you'll need to scale down what I suggest, and those incidences (and how you need to adjust them) will be clear to you.

The Internet (and the Web in particular) has brought opportunity to the independent creator like no other invention prior. Our ability to publish our work and reach a potential audience of millions has changed the landscape of content provision markedly and permanently. But, with this opportunity comes a responsibility that we each learn how to be not only good creators, but good businesspeople as well. It has long been the tradition that when a creator signed on with a big distributor (record label, syndicate, and so on), the creator would just create and the distributor (effectively the commercial partner) would deal with the business of business. This tradition has, sadly, kept most of the creator pool exactly where the distributors want them: in the dark when it comes to business dealings. With the advent of the Web and the rise of the independent creator, it behooves us to take all of our interests in our own hands—because if we don't, others will supersede our interests with their own.

That you're reading this book already speaks volumes about your desire to become a financially responsible and successful creator, and that you're compelled to take the rudder instead of letting someone else do it for you. For this, I congratulate you. When you've finished the book, you'll be armed with the knowledge you need to set up the pieces you need to get the money flowing toward you in exchange for your hard work. If you're someone who'd like to make a living as a creator, you'll also know what you need to do to get there.

I feel very fortunate that I've been able to work my way through the last several years as a cartoonist, without being shackled to a traditional syndication contract. It means that I can do what I love every day, and interact with the interesting people who come to see what I have to say as a creator. It also means that there is clearly room for independent content providers who don't play the game by the rules that most of the Big Guys want us to play by.

The content landscape has changed a great deal in the past ten years, in ways that demand our attention. If opportunities are just waiting to be plucked, what's stopping us from doing so? I have always believed that a vista filled with independents gives all of us more strength and variety, choices that aren't limited to what the large syndicates of whatever stripe present to us as consumers. For that reason, to me, nothing would be more satisfying than to see hundreds if not thousands of new faces on the Web, plying their talent and earning a living, all on their own and without the say-so of a Daddy Warbucks.

Start reading and go get 'em!

JD "Illiad" Frazer
Vancouver, B.C., Canada

Acknowledgments

I began teaching other creators about the online world only because I was well taught by others who are wiser than me. I hate writing acknowledgments; I have learned so much from so many people that I just *know* I will neglect to mention someone of importance. If so, you have my humble apologies in advance.

This book would never have been started had I not been wisely advised by Barry Carlson, my business mentor, to put the early scrawls that were *User Friendly* on the Web.

The moderators of my forum deserve my deep gratitude for helping me with a very difficult job. In particular, Greg "Kickstart" Webster and a moderator who shall only be known as "Nea" have my thanks for sticking by me and offering valuable perspectives for all this time.

My thanks to "Ravenlock" and "bitflipper," two much-respected members of the UF community who generously offered their thoughtful perspectives on the issue of social ethics in an online world. I really do have some great readers.

I get a gentle and much needed kick in the can periodically from someone I deem the best agent in the business. David Fugate, my book agent, was instrumental in getting me published from day one. He also gets a thank-you for putting me together with the very fine folks at Wiley.

Speaking of which, Kevin Shafer, my development editor at Wiley, helped this beginning writer look better than I probably deserve. He also stayed calm under some heavy deadlines. He must have godlike control of his adrenal gland.

And also Chris Webb, the head editorial honcho over at Wiley. Sir, I appreciate the faith you have in me and the opportunities you are so willing to provide creators like myself. We need more executive editors with your outlook.

Much gratitude goes to Ken "Caesar" Fisher for being my technical reviewer. I've long been a fan of Ken's work over at Ars Technica, and felt that someone like him would have the critical eye needed to poke at the weak parts of the book. He did, and then some. It is thanks to him that I was able to reinforce what needed reinforcing.

I would be terribly remiss if I didn't acknowledge the important contributions offered by Dr. David Greenwald, and Mark "dire lobo" Suazo, experts in their fields and people whom I have developed much respect for their views on online socializing. These two taught me a great deal about human motivations.

Finally, it wouldn't be right if I didn't mention David "Smiling Man" Barton, the guy who handles all of the tangled ink and paper that comes with running a business, particularly a business in the creative industry. I'd still be drawing cartoons on the backs of nappies if it weren't for his timely and potent business guidance. All creators need a friend like him. Thanks, man!

Introduction

The Web today is overrun with personal pages, collections of photos, amateur artwork and music, and above all, blogs. Blogs are everywhere, and anyone can get one. It's easier to have your writing and other personal content published on the Web today than ever before.

A constant dream of a great many people is being able to make a living from their creative work. Most everyone fancies themselves a writer, or journalist, or photographer, or visual artist. With the recent rise in the "creative class," it's clear that the world is once again ready to allow for the talented and dedicated to carve out a self-made career online as a content creator. But being creative isn't enough. Today's content creators must tangle with the labyrinthine business of earning revenue from their work. The Web has enabled anyone to publish their cartoon, column, or music without having to earn the blessings of a syndicate or record label, which puts more power in the hands of the creators. At the same time, the creators must accept the considerable responsibility of promoting and monetizing their product.

What This Book Covers

This book addresses a clear need in the instructional market today. While there are any number of books on creativity, writing, illustration, and self-expression, there is very little out there that tackles the thorny subject of making money for these pursuits. Given the number of people who strive very hard to rise above the morass of mediocre content on the Web, and given the common dream of making a living as a member of the creative class, this book is for readers who are clearly motivated by their very personal career dreams.

Like so many people who even now are pursuing careers as creators, you probably (at best) have a vague inkling about the ways that people can make money by publishing online content. Rather than offer nebulous promises of vast wealth, this book teaches you how to build and run a sustainable content business and make a living from it. This isn't a book about celebrity—it's about practical business methods and understanding the dynamic and value of an online audience.

Any book about online content also must tackle the issue of intellectual property and creator rights and ethics, particularly given the nature of the medium, one in which it is shockingly easy to rip off a creator. This book covers the seemingly tricky (but actually simple) set of decisions each creator must make, decisions that need to be realistic in a world where enforcement is often expensive and difficult.

Given that a creator's central monetization asset is his or her audience, the subject of online community building and maintenance is integral to the business picture. Books that explain the philosophy and practice of online community building— social computing—by their nature don't address the commercial facet. Within the context of this book, however, this is not only expected, but necessary. You will be taught how to approach the subject of monetizing your audience without alienating them, again with sustainability for the long-term in mind.

This book includes anecdotal and historical information that the Web-using public will find compelling. Readers like to see successful stories, especially in areas that they wish to pursue themselves. Examples include the author's experience with Userfriendly.org and Ars Technica, both amateur efforts that grew into worldwide successes on the Web.

Who This Book Is For

This book addresses the following readership niches:

- A business primer for established creative professionals seeking to bring their work from the "Old World" to the Web

- A guide and reference for aspiring members of the creative class who wish to build a business out of their creative efforts

- A guidebook for companies with an online presence that would like to initiate and eventually monetize a "consumer audience" or community

- A reference for content providers who must face ethical considerations in online business decisions

- An entertaining read for anyone with an interest in the fascinating workings of online commerce and the market forces that shape it

How This Book Is Structured

This book consists of ten chapters and an appendix, organized as follows:

- *Chapter 1, "The Business of Creating Content"*—This chapter covers the history of the creative class, from the ancient days (when having a wealthy patron was required to be a full-time artist) to the modern world (where, thanks to globalization, you can earn a living by entertaining the masses). This chapter also covers the fundamental problems faced by all creators, and the usual naivete that runs rampant among the class. This is followed by an explanation of the syndication game, its strengths, pitfalls, past and future; how syndicates and record labels are the same; how the "creator's pyramid" or "food-chain" works; and the realities of self-syndication.

- *Chapter 2, "The Advertising Game"*—This chapter covers the advertising business model as a whole, starting off with a brief history of advertising and its success as a revenue stream. This is reinforced by the importance of understanding the demographics of your audience, and the value in building a media kit. Next is a section on print advertising and how it differs from the Web, both positive and negative aspects. This is followed by a discussion of several Web advertising methods, including static ads, pop-ups and pop-unders, eye-blasters, interstitials, text ads, and e-mail advertising, with an examination of the short- and long-term benefits and disadvantages of each. Finally, and perhaps most importantly, this chapter includes a discussion of how to generate a steady stream of money from the advertising business model.

- *Chapter 3, "The Membership Game"*—This chapter addresses the business model of charging money for access to, or advanced features of, the content on a Web site. This includes the psychology of online consumers and how to attract their hard-earned dollars with offers and arguments other than "you should pay for this," plus how to make it easy and obvious for your audience to give you money. This chapter includes a follow-up discussion of how to generate steady revenue from the membership business model.

- *Chapter 4, "To Gate or Not to Gate"*—The chapter opens by covering the philosophies of Exclusivity and Inclusivity in content on the Web. This includes an explanation of how Exclusivity (gating off content to paying members only) can be a powerful draw. On the flip side, this chapter includes a discussion of how Inclusivity (allowing access to everyone with no monetary transactions) gives a creator reach. The chapter concludes with coverage on finding that "happy middle ground" or magic point on the graph where the most revenue is derived.

- *Chapter 5, "Branding and Merchandising"*—This chapter addresses the power behind established brands, and how to use your brand to generate more revenue. This includes a discussion on the benefits and dangers of endorsements and partnerships on the Web, as well as the principle of using your art to promote your art. The discussion covers royalties and merchandising, the revenue opportunities, and the business pitfalls and benefits of putting your brand on commodities and products.

- *Chapter 6, "Online Communities and Online Consumers"*—Covering the difference between a consumer base and a community, this chapter addresses the demands of an online consumer base and the immense value intrinsic to the direct connection between a creator and his or her audience. The principles of real versus online versus distributed communities and their importance to an online creator are discussed. The chapter also covers the many considerations in initiating and running a successful online community, including the complex and difficult world of writing behavior policies. The chapter concludes with a section regarding the revenue value of online communities.

- *Chapter 7, "The Ethics of Creation and Consumption"*—This chapter talks about the ethics that exist between a creator and his or her audience, both overt and implied. The history of content on the Web and the way it has been consumed over the years is addressed, and the shift in the mental and political climate over this charged issue is discussed. Finally, a conclusion around the basic idea that "There Ain't No Such Thing As A Free Lunch" (TANSTAAFL) is explored, especially with regard to the long-term consequences if the audience at large doesn't cease the practice of content thievery.

- *Chapter 8, "Protecting Your Creation"*—This chapter addresses copyright law and trademark law, and when none, one, or both are necessary in protecting your work. Following the discussion in Chapter 7 on ethics of creation and consumption, this chapter also details the four major consumer personalities on the Web: the Thief, the Naïve, the Policeman, and the Citizen.

- *Chapter 9, "Fame and Your Audience"*—This chapter covers a problem a lot of creators wished they had: fame. Although it can be a useful thing to have, fame comes with a plethora of unpleasant issues that the unprepared will have to face. This includes the problem of losing sight of the forest for the trees, and building an Ivory Tower and cutting yourself off from your audience. This chapter also discusses the other side of fame, where self-esteem can take a daily beating, and how to remain centered and focused on the reality of the situation.

- *Chapter 10, "Ready, Fire, Aim!"*—This chapter concludes the book by restating general principles and goals.

- *Appendix A, "References and Resources"*—This appendix offers a springboard list of online resources that will help creative entrepreneurs with information and offer forums for them to share their ideas and experiences.

Contents

· ·

Money for Content and Your Clicks for Free: Turning Web Sites, Blogs, and Podcasts Into Cash

chapter

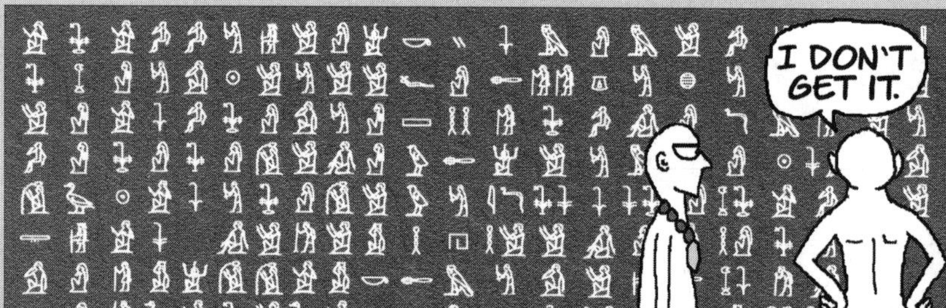
I DON'T GET IT.
ddp

The Business of Creating Content

You have brains in your head.

You have feet in your shoes.

You can steer yourself any direction you choose.

— *Dr. Seuss*

I had always wanted to be a writer of some sort — fiction, preferably, taking the form of a screenplay, a script, a novel, a short story anthology, fairy tales, whatever. I knew this when I was barely out of my larval stage, say around six years. I had always thought it was just *so cool* that there were people in this world who spent all day, every day, writing stories for other people. It was like being a tiny, flawed god of a sort, creating worlds and inviting other people to explore them.

Of course, by the time I was getting into my cocoon stage — adolescence — real life began to intrude. I still had romantic notions of becoming a writer, but there was a part of my brain (likely the part that was concerned with such bad habits as eating and staying warm) that kept nagging at me. "Oi," it would say, "what are you going to do about rent then? And beer. And some good nosh. Perhaps you can drop the rent, but the beer and nosh are a must."

Modern 14-year-olds aren't usually too cognizant of the realities of earning a living. Most of the time, they're exclusively focused on the latest electronics, television program, music, and/or the appropriate gender. Although I was an unequivocal geek during junior high school and mucked about with a big cranky Hewlett Packard 2000 and was generally an inquisitive sort, I really had no clue about such mundane things as mortgages and grocery bills.

As most people are wont to do (pubescent or otherwise), I glossed over all of the "boring parts" of writing as a career. I had in my mind an appealing image of myself hunched over a keyboard, a hot cup of chai latte on my antique desk, in a warmly decorated room that was clearly part of an expensive — but not expensive for me! — log home located somewhere near the water amidst lots of evergreen trees. I would write brilliantly and money would just *roll* in, enough money to afford me my dream home and allow me to dress in an eccentric manner (galoshes and corduroy, for example).

Fast forward 20 years. I had written quite a lot in that time, and some of it was even fiction. Some of it was even published. And some of that I was even paid for.

I'm still waiting on the log home.

This isn't to say that I haven't found some measure of success. I make a decent living as a cartoonist, and have been for more than six years as of this writing. I don't have an expensive log home on the water, but I do bring in enough money to afford me a roof over my head, food, heat, the occasional latte, and if I really want them, galoshes and all the corduroy I could wear. I'll wait on the latter until I'm well ensconced in a white cedar house.

All of this is just a roundabout way of saying that the writing or painting or cartooning or whatever it is that you do as a creative person is the "easy" part of the equation. It's easy — at least it *should be* — because it's known; it's something you have passion for and drive to do. The "hard," unknown part is making money from your creativity. How do you extract dollars out of your art?

That question was always in the background for me. When I was around 19 years of age, I had finished writing a short story with which I was quite pleased. It had a moral, a dynamic character, and read like a parable. It wasn't particularly sophisticated, but it was mine, and I had polished it carefully over a few months, making sure the grammar was impeccable and that the story itself was engaging and readable. "Ha!" I gloated to myself, "Riches now await me!"

At which point I scratched my head and wondered what the heck to do next.

The traditional method of getting paid for something like a short story involves a publisher. (This clearly remains a valid way of earning some coin for your art, or else you wouldn't be reading this book.) So, I did what most writers do: I told myself that no publisher would want to buy my work, but that's okay, because my work was too good for them! I proudly shelved my masterpiece and it eventually ended up where it truly deserved, as tinder for the fireplace.

This isn't to say that I think my work was horrid; rather, I'm using the story to illustrate how creative people love to create, but really would rather not do the part that involves taking, say, a manuscript and translating it into dollars. We all think there should be an inconspicuous (yet convenient) drop box somewhere that allows us to insert our brilliance. From this drop box comes a token, and with this token we go to a similarly inconspicuous (yet convenient) vending machine and from it we buy, say, a log home. Wouldn't that be grand?

Grand as it may be, vending machines with log homes are not reality. I had somewhat come to terms with this by the time I was 21. During my years in high school, I had spent many of my waking hours cartooning, doodling, and making satirical comments about my classmates and teachers. I also had the naïve dream — sibling to my dream of writing — that I could perhaps make a career out of cartooning. So, I diligently produced a dozen comic strips (titled "Dust Puppies") and sent copies off to the six biggest comic strip syndicates in North America.

The result was predictable. Six submissions replied to with six rejection letters. I'm sure I still have them somewhere, perhaps lining the bottom of an underwear drawer.

It was a strange thing, receiving the rejections. I remember opening the first reply (I believe it was from King Features Syndicate), feeling anxious. Oddly, when I saw it was a rejection I was *relieved*. A friend of mine who majored in psychology suggested it was because I loved the idea of being a cartoonist, but didn't really want the responsibility of earning a living from it. Looking back on that day, I think I'd have to say she was absolutely right.

There is a pervasive naivete in creative people. We're full of verve and fire when we're doing what we love, talking about those things that make our eyes gleam maniacally. At the same time, we brush aside the things we don't understand, such as the business of making money. We do this because creative people are often psychologically similar to children. Given a choice, most of us would rather be locked away in a comfy room somewhere with all of our tools and toys, producing what we do, and oblivious to all of the paperwork and money that changes hands outside of that room. We'd also expect some of that money to come our way, but if the businesspeople outside our comfy room, our "parents" so to speak, shoved a pizza under the door every now and then, we'd be just fine.

Consider this perspective:

> *"Perhaps it is the different parts of the brain or some other such dichotomy: left brain/right brain, logical/creative, math mind/artistic mind, details/big picture, new stimuli/routine. Or maybe it is that the creative part of the brain is from the "child" within. Children learn a great deal of things that are new, are very creative and artistic, and enjoy "play," including mind or word play. Creative people are often able to be able to display those attributes, and may "specialize" in those abilities.*

"Another aspect is that creativity and coding are often solitary activities, whereas business meetings are just that, meetings. Socializing may be problematic for a variety of people for various reasons. Some people have social anxiety and just avoid all social contact. Others avoid areas where they may appear not at the top of their game. Some people have difficulty with the discipline of orderly, structured, task-oriented business sessions. Some people have trouble with math and the details of paying attention to numbers and plans.

"Many creative people are used to having the power of their own actions remain in their hands. Meetings function on consensus, or are certainly slower than individual decisions. At meetings, everyone needs to get their say, and this makes the process slow and cumbersome for a person used to quick results. The ideas of others, especially those whose ideas seem not very worthwhile, can provoke impatience and boredom.

"But many creative people are just not very interested in business issues. The creative mind is interested in coming up with new, unique solutions. Business and monetary considerations are fairly tried and true. Formulae are not particularly creative. Also, it may be more fun to "give forth" and express than to hoard and control and maintain. Control can be an important consideration.

"Essentially, I guess it comes down to the nature of play and the nature of work. Creative people are often people who have found a way to make their lives more playful: coding, inventing, gaming, cartooning, discussing dreams, reading, and so forth, worrying about monetary concerns. And it does come down to worry for most of us (there are those entrepreneurs who seem to find making money a playful activity) as it is not play, it is work! Play is the realm of the child, the id, the irrational; business is the realm of the parent, the ego/superego, the rational. It is best when these so-called divisions are balanced and blended, but we all have our limits."

— Dr. David Greenwald, Clinical Psychologist and Partner at `Speak2docs.com`

This naïve outlook is what differentiates the creative amateur from the creative professional. The professional not only plies his or her talent, but also accepts the responsibility of handling all of the difficult, mundane (yet necessary) aspects of earning a living from his or her art. "Handling it" may simply involve hiring someone whom he or she trusts to do it for him or her, but any professional also keeps an eye on the job being done. If you want to make the most money you can from your work, you'd best be prepared to learn the fundamentals of the business world. That way, even if you've hired a business expert to maximize your earnings, you can still understand what's going on outside of your own "comfy room."

This is perhaps one of the most difficult truths for aspiring creative types to face: Earning a living (or even just a few dollars) from being creative requires *effort*. It isn't always easy, and there'll always be a task you don't like doing that must be done. The glamour of which you dream and the romantic notions you have are usually just that: dreams and notions. Creative work is fulfilling, no question, but note that it is called creative *work*.

Consider this:

> *"[I]t's easy to be an author, whether of fiction or nonfiction, and it's a pleasant profession. Fiction authors go about making speeches and signing books. Computer authors go to computer shows and then come home to open boxes of new equipment and software, and play with the new stuff until they tire of it. It's nice work if you can get it.*

> *"The problem is that no one pays you to be an author.*

> *"To be an author, you must first be a writer; and while it's easy to be an author, being a writer is hard work. Surprisingly, it may be only hard work; that is, while some people certainly have more talent for writing than others, everyone has some. The good news is that nearly anyone who wants to badly enough can make some kind of living at writing. The bad news is that wanting to badly enough means being willing to devote the time and work necessary to learn the trade.*

> *"The secret of becoming a writer is that you have to write. You have to write a lot. You also have to finish what you write, even though no one wants it yet. If you don't learn to finish your work, no one will ever want to see it. The biggest mistake new writers make is carrying around copies of unfinished work to inflict on their friends.*

> *"I am sure it has been done with less, but you should be prepared to write and throw away a million words of finished material. By finished, I mean completed, done, ready to submit, and written as well as you know how at the time you wrote it. You may be ashamed of it later, but that's another story."*

> — *Jerry Pournelle, co-author (and writer!) of Lucifer's Hammer, Footfall, and a plethora of other really great science fiction novels.*

Let's assume you either don't have this problem, or you're willing to do those ordinary tasks that vex us creative types so much, sacrificing your "artistic innocence" so that you can put bread on the table. You understand the utility and necessity of accountants, lawyers, contracts, intellectual property laws, and all of those elements without which our world would have fewer shades of grey. You have all the tools and basic skills required of a writer, illustrator, cartoonist, journalist, whatever.

This brings us to the killer question: do you really have what it takes to be a creative professional and a member of what has been labeled the "creative class"?

First, what exactly is the "creative class"?

Most people will answer that it is the sector of the populace that makes a living from their creativity. They are the professionals in the creative industries, which includes filmmaking, social commentators, writing novels, musicians, advertising, cartooning, and all of those careers that involve both creation and expression of some kind. Whether or not this group actually exists as a "class" in what we assume is supposed to be a classless society is a topic for sociologists to argue. Perhaps a more politically correct (PC) classification would be "creative professions"; for the sake of simplicity, I'll use "creative class" to describe "the demographic that includes people who derive income by applying their creative abilities in the production of media that others might enjoy."

I knew that I very much wanted to become a member of this professional group. What I didn't know was whether or not I had what it took to actually make a real go of it. I enjoy making people think and laugh, so cartooning seemed the most obvious route to follow. I learned, the hard way, that cartooning is probably the most consistently difficult form of creative expression to accomplish.

Consider this:

> "[W]hat truly confounds me is how some people resent cartoonists taking a vacation. But I'm assuming that those are people who know the least about cartooning. We are the only ones in all of media whose work appears every day. If you think it's no big deal, get out 365 sheets of paper and fill them up with new, completely original cartoons. And when you're done with that, get out 365 more sheets. And repeat this every year for the rest of your life."
>
> — Wiley Miller, creator of the comic strip Non Sequitur, rec.arts.comics.strips, (June 12, 1998)

Luckily for me, I didn't read Miller's words of wisdom before diving into the realm of cartooning. Miller is a respected, successful comic strip author syndicated by Universal Press Syndicate and the only two-category award winner in the National Cartoonists Society. He knows of what he speaks in this matter, and I'm sure I would've been intimidated by his description of a cartoonist's life.

As it turns out, I discovered that I do have what it takes to be a professional cartoonist. I ended up, several years after having what was left of my ego crushed by the syndicates, publishing *User Friendly* online for all of my friends to read. In less than two years I went from an audience of 20 friends and associates to an audience of more than a million people around the world. And I did it without a syndicate's blessings.

There remained a problem: I had a huge readership, but I wasn't making any money. I had a full-time job, but with a very busy Web site and the demands of a daily cartoon, I found that I had little time for sleep, much less anything else. I realized at that point that I would have to do the one thing that everyone who wants to make a living on their own as a creative professional must do: take the plunge and make creating my full-time job.

(As an aside, if you have no intentions of blogging or podcasting or cartooning full-time, you're not alone. There are millions of people who would like to just make a few dollars on the side with their creativity and perspective, enough to buy some beer or maybe the latest video card. You have a full-time job you love and your blogging alter-ego, and that's perfectly fine. But read this section anyway, it'll help you with assessing what you might be able to do in the future.)

To be a successful working member of the creative class, you'll need to understand and adopt a particular attitude and set of guidelines. You'll also probably need to disabuse yourself of some of the more rampant myths of working as a creative professional.

The Good, the Bad, and the Fake

Myth #1: Working for yourself has to be easier than working for someone else.

I hear this one all of the time, usually from people who have managers that are apparently first-generation clones of Attila the Hun. The truth is that it can be easier in some ways, but much more difficult than others. It's easier because your commute, assuming you work from home, is all of ten seconds from your bed to your desk. It's easier because you don't have to contend with public transit, traffic, or bad weather. It's also easier because you can, if you really want to, work naked.

But it's more difficult because you are your only taskmaster. You might decide to slack off a bit, only to face the cold shock of seeing a bill and YIKES! You haven't made *any* money in the last two weeks with which you can pay that bill. It's more difficult because you never really have "weekends" like the rest of the world. While your mates are out quaffing ale and beer at the local watering hole, you're slaving away over the latest podcast or blog entry. It's more difficult because after five o'clock, it's unlikely you can just "call it a day" and leave all of your work behind. You live, breathe, and dream your work, every day, every hour, even when you're on vacation.

Myth #2: Independent creative professionals make money hand over fist.

I make my living as a humorist, and I swear to Zeus I can't think of a single statement that's funnier than that one. Every time I hear it I can barely survive the
pain in my sides. In fact, I have to change my pants just because it's on the page
I'm writing at this moment.

Now, this isn't to say that members of the creative class can't make a fortune, but
the odds of doing so are up there with becoming the next Tom Cruise, Sara
Maclachlan, or Charlize Theron. You can realistically make anywhere between a
modest to a decent living. Just don't swallow the lie that this industry is where you
will make a king's ransom.

Myth #3: Joining the creative class is a great way to obtain adoration and recognition.

This one is almost as funny as Myth #2. If you're the kind of person who gets a
charge out of being famous and you seek that in this profession, I *highly* recommend you consider a career waiting tables. You'll have a better chance of achieving
public recognition there than you will working as a Web-based independent creative
professional. This is because on the Web, your audience is potentially worldwide.
Although you may earn an enthusiastic fan base in, say, Latvia, if you're based in
Saskatchewan you're not likely to meet very many of them.

On the other hand, the Internet does permit that same global audience to write to
you much more readily. You'll begin receiving e-mail from complete strangers, many
of whom will like or love what you do, whether it's music, cartooning, podcasting,
and so on. If that kind of recognition is enough for you, then this gig is probably
for you.

Keep in mind, however, that you'll also be opening the door to hate mail. The
same medium that makes you so accessible to your fans also makes it trivial for
someone with an anti-you agenda to vent their spleen directly into your mailbox.

Myth #4: Being creative is easy. Anyone can do it.

Then why doesn't everyone do it?

It's because being creative every day, 365 days a year with a bonus day thrown in
every leap year, is not easy. You have to be talented or dedicated, and preferably
both. Wiley Miller's comment about filling 365 blank pages with original, funny
cartoons every year illustrates this well. The same can be said for writing a newspaper column, or creating weekly podcasts. Some creative energy has to go into
every single incarnation of your work that you do, and the creative well isn't
always full. When the well runs dry, it's dry, and it has to be refilled.

Unfortunately, the days keep ticking on at a regular pace. If your well is dry when the next day or week rolls around and you don't have a cartoon, column, or podcast ready to go, you look pretty silly, not to mention unprofessional.

Not just anyone can be a creative professional, particularly an independent one on the Web.

There's a little more to this. Not everyone has the *talent* to be a creative professional either. Maybe you draw cartoons or write stories and your family and friends all tell you that they're very good. That's a plus for sure, but keep in mind that Mom and Dad are *supposed* to love you. They aren't the best critics of your work, and probably won't be able to give you an honest, useful assessment. If an unbiased critic (someone who has little to lose when they tell you something unpleasant) informs you that your work is really quite smashing, you have a good indication that your talents do indeed lie in the field you have chosen.

What to Look Forward to

Now that I've busted the most common myths having to do with the creative class, let's cover the plusses of being a creative professional, things you can look forward to realistically.

Boon #1: Your Time Is Your Own

Another way of saying that is you work to your own schedule. You can ditch the 9-to-5 fetters and choose when it is you want to work. There is a not-insignificant percentage of the population that does their best work between the hours of 10:00 p.m. and dawn. Sleep during the day, get up in the afternoon, and ply your trade at night—that's up to you! The only real restriction you face is the dreaded deadline. Provided you can work to them, you get to choose what hours of the day you do your creating.

Of course, if you need to get in touch with people who have standard 9-to-5 hours, you'll have to make yourself available as required. This is less likely to be an issue early on in the game, but as you establish your business and you form commercial relationships, adjusting your schedule from time to time will be necessary.

Boon #2: You're in Your Element

You get to do what you love for money. You'll leave behind the manacles of the wage-slave, no longer at the mercy of some petty, egocentric boss who wants you to perform superhuman feats at the office doing something you don't love doing, all the while letting him or her take the credit and paying you less than you're worth. If you love to expound on political issues, you get to do that on a regular basis, and people will pay you for it. Not only is it (mostly) fun and fulfilling, it's something that will probably help you grow as a person.

Boon #3: No More Workplace Politics

Anyone who has had to work with other people knows that wherever there are co-workers, there will be a clash of agendas. In the workplace, the most common clash is over privilege and resources — promotions, wages, and futures. Treachery and petty in-fighting are common elements of the workplace. A jealous co-worker could file a sexual harassment suit against you just because he or she thinks it'll help to win that promotion because you'll be out of the way. Overall, working in the modern corporation really quite sucks the big one.

Working for yourself means that you'll never have to deal with this. You'll have competition, but that's part of trading in a free market. What you won't have is some psychotic or emotionally dysfunctional co-worker watching your every move, looking for a gap between which he or she can slip a metaphorical dagger. Also, you won't have to worry about promotion — you're *it*, the boss, the head honcho. There are no higher ranks for you to attain within your own company. Your payback will take the form of accomplishments, some recognition, and most importantly for living, money.

Boon #4: You Can Change Someone's Life

Your impact as a member of the creative class shouldn't be underestimated. People affect other people every day just by interacting with them for the briefest moments. A kind smile from a stranger may lift someone out of a bout of depression; a terse, angry word could enrage an otherwise peaceful person; a thumbs-up from a co-worker could boost your confidence by an order of magnitude.

Creative professionals on the Web have the ability to do much more, to effect greater change, largely because they distill moments like these into art, photography, writing, cartoons, music, whatever, and make it available to the rest of the Web. A podcaster who is politically astute and eloquent can sway the minds of hundreds, if not thousands of voters. A blogger can write an appeal for aid to a little-known town in some hinterland and drive financial as well as moral support to the town's inhabitants. The Web enables each of us to reach an audience far larger and far more diverse than we ever could have before, no longer limited by the networks and channels created by the syndicates and their brethren.

And, if nothing else, you'll change your life by joining the creative class, hopefully for the better.

What Not to Look Forward to

So that's all the good stuff in a nutshell. But where there is light, there is shadow; where there is liquid nitrogen, there is some dork who doesn't know how badly he or she can get into trouble with the stuff. There are distinct disadvantages to the creative class. And they're all pretty bad.

Thing that Sucks #1: Your Time May Be Yours, But It's Highly Limited

It's a good thing your commute in the morning is only ten seconds. It's a very good thing that you're able to work all hours of the day, because odds are, you just might.

I face a deadline every day, in a manner of speaking. I have made an implicit contract with my audience that I will provide one cartoon a day, every day, 365 days a year without fail. The cartoon updates at midnight, Pacific Time. *User Friendly's* universe encompasses geekdom and topical events that occur in the world of technology, gaming, and all of those other odd elements that make up the Geek gestalt.

As a result, I have to keep up on current events. I spend roughly two hours every day reading up on the latest developments in the tech world, their ramifications to society and the law, and so on, and so forth, *ad infinitum*. Rendering a cartoon takes anywhere between half an hour to four hours, depending on the mechanical complexity. *Writing* the cartoon. . . ah, now that can take five seconds or it can take forever.

The essence of cartooning — at least in *User Friendly's* case — is in the writing. I could have a terrific topic to satirize, but if I can't put my finger on quite the right words, I may flounder for hours, staring at a blank screen. On the other hand, the writing could be so obvious to me that I just scrawl a rough note down and fine-tune the words after I've drawn the cartoon.

The thing of it is, when midnight rolls around, it makes no difference to the world if I've spent eight hours on the upcoming cartoon or eight minutes; they expect a cartoon, and I've promised it to them.

As I've mentioned before, when the well runs dry, all you're going to drink is sand. So, I've learned to work like a tenant farmer in medieval England while the well is full, pumping out three, four, nine cartoons a day (my record for one day is eleven). When it's dry, I do other things, like administration, banking, that sort of thing. I do this because I don't want to be caught at 11:47 P.M., no cartoon in hand and no ideas for one either.

This is what I mean by your time being "highly limited." You must always use it as best as you're able, or you'll end up with no end of grief. A creative professional who misses too many deadlines doesn't remain a creative professional for long.

Thing that Sucks #2: Only the Lonely

For a lot of people who dream of working from home for themselves, loneliness never enters their mind. Once they realize their dream, they suddenly realize how much they miss the social aspects of a workplace.

This isn't a disadvantage to me; I rate very high on the introvert scale and very much enjoy working entirely on my own. This doesn't mean I can't work with groups. I used to be a project manager and a pretty good one if I do say so myself. But given a choice, I'd rather work on my own in a quiet room with a cup of tea and piles of books surrounding me. My productivity is generally very high in that kind of environment, largely because I'm not interrupted.

But I do understand that for a great many people, perhaps even most, human contact in the workplace is quite necessary. My business development guy (I have my very own Smiling Man — *User Friendly* readers will understand the reference) is hard-working, dedicated, talented, and. . . loves the company of others. He works at home as I do, and has expressed to me a few times how much he misses working next to others. I imagine this is a common concern, and one that isn't easily solved.

If you suspect you'll go stark-raving mad if you were to work entirely on your own, you might want to think about working in a shared office, or perhaps consider a different career path. The truth is that in this industry working alone is not that uncommon.

Thing that Sucks #3: The Regular Paycheck Becomes a Creature of Myth

There is something to be said for knowing that you'll be receiving a check for a fixed, predictable amount on the 15th and the 30th of every month. You can reliably plan for paying your mortgage, vacations, shopping trips, all of those things that make life a little more bearable.

In the world of the creative class, the creature known as "the regular paycheck" is a bit of a white rabbit. It's usually late, it's very hard to catch, and the stupid thing often ends up down some hole. Pay, in this line of work, can be very sporadic. However, play your cards right and the pay can come in a constant, if irregular, stream. I'll explain more about that in Chapter 2.

It took me several months of gliding on my savings — such as they were — before the money started coming in for *User Friendly*. Given the state of the Web today, you have the ability to avoid some risk if you start out part-time and then move on into full-time. The drawback is, of course, that part-time efforts usually yield part-time results. When you have no safety net, such as the one provided by a regular paycheck at your day job, your mind switches into financial-survival mode. You'll probably become more aggressive and more driven, and your full-time efforts will show in your work.

Thing that Sucks #4: The Buck, She Stops Here

You are the boss, which means that you have no one else to blame if you fail. If the market becomes tough and you implode, it's because you failed to adapt. If a competitor comes along and renders all of your work redundant, it's because you failed to keep up your work quality. Ultimately, you can blame anyone or anything you like if you fail, but no one else is going to listen. There will be no higher authority for you to appeal to, unless you're religious, and even then it's doubtful that your God will let you blame Him.

What this also means is that it's up to you to figure out ways to make what you do a financial success. You have to find the paying customers and fulfill your obligations. You have to decide on which investments in time and money are the right ones for your own future as a creative professional. If you don't find the customers, it doesn't matter how talented you are; it's hard to eat or seek shelter under a blog, cartoon, or podcast.

If none of the things that suck have dissuaded you, you're a) determined, b) incredibly naïve, or c) insane. I'll put a fiver on the last choice. It seems to run in this particular sector of society.

You have the upsides, the downsides, and the truth behind the myths. The next thing to cover is the history of the creative professional and why it matters to us today.

When Was the First "Content Provider" Born?

No one really knows, but it's clear from pictographs found on cave walls that telling stories and recording them were always important human activities, even during the time of the caveman. There can be little doubt that there had been times around the caveman campfire when the story of that really big, fat hairy mammoth that got away was told, and in each telling you can bet the mammoth got bigger. (Had it not been for fossil records, the skeptic in me would've suspected that "mammoths" were probably only six inches tall and cavemen hunted them and put them on shish-kebabs four at a time.) What we don't know is whether or not the caveman storyteller was given any sort of compensation for the entertainment he provided. I would guess "yes" because oral historians in today's aboriginal tribes are granted a place of honor and are often supported by the rest of the tribe to maintain and teach the mental trove of stories about their peoples.

The Ancients Were Sure Into It

A bit ahead of the cavemen were the Gauls and Britons. These peoples had Druids, a class of their society that judged, advised kings, and, among many other things, taught morals with stories and kept their oral histories.

The Bards, the lowest rank of Druids, were the poets and storytellers. They learned, recited, and contributed to the oral history. They also composed epic stories that they told to their tribe and others; this was the equivalent to the feature film of the modern world. Bards were supported by their tribe when they were home, and were paid in coin and food when they traveled.

The Middle Ages and Renaissance Aren't to Be Outdone

Creative people did span the ages, and they did some remarkable work in medieval times. Consider the Bayeux Tapestry, a glorious visual representation of the Battle of Hastings, one of the pivotal points in English history. In effect, it's like cartooning, using images and words to tell a story.

In medieval Europe, most writing was ecclesiastical in nature. Monks devoted their entire lives to producing and copying religious writings in very expensive books — expensive because the pages were made from parchment (split sheepskin) or vellum (calfskin). A single large book such as the Holy Bible required as many as 170 calfskins or 300 sheepskins, a considerable expense in resources for the medium alone. Once you add in the cost of a trained monastic illuminator and the inks used, a single book was a treasure that only the Church, wealthy merchants, or the nobility could readily afford. These "writers" (the highly trained monks) were supported by the Church.

Along comes printing with movable metal type, which was perfected in Mainz by around 1450. By the time of Gutenberg's youth, paper (created from pulped fibers as opposed to animal skins) was plentiful and about one-sixth the price of parchment. (Vellum and parchment were still used for the sake of magnificence; a printer would use vellum for important works and documents, for example.)

Printed books took a little time to appear in great numbers, and most of the first ones remained religious in nature, or were brief guides to living and dying well. Secular works were predominately stories of chivalry and moral behavior. But this became the time when the printed word would explode. By 1500, the presses in Europe had produced some 6 million copies in 40,000 editions, likely more books than were published in Western Europe since the fall of Rome!

Thinkers became writers, and new thought spread across Europe several orders of magnitude faster than before the printed word. These writers weren't all ecclesiastical, and they could make a variable living from their words. The most successful did very well indeed, such as the sixteenth-century Italian humanist Niccolo Machiavelli. His *Discourses on Livy* and *The Prince* weren't enormous, epic works, but they were read so widely by the nobility and politicians of the day that his work was to influence politics for the next 400 years.

Fast-forward to the twentieth century. Books since the Renaissance have evolved from being purely religious treasures into a vehicle of all human thought and expression. Everything from guides to encyclopedias to entertaining stories fill the pages between the many covers, and today's audiences pay in hard currency for access to this content. In the 1930s, it was still possible to make a decent living writing fiction, as H.P. Lovecraft's contemporaries proved. Lovecraft himself died penniless, mostly because he was vastly better at writing than he was at being concerned with making money, a fate this book will help you avoid.

Printed books solved the problems of costly production and distribution; what it did not solve is the difficulty of getting published. The average writer does not have the resources to edit, print, bind, market, and distribute his or her own work, all tasks that are handled by a centralizing body, the publisher. Publishers, like any other business, exist to make a profit. Clearly they cannot publish every manuscript (or even every good manuscript) that arrives on their doorsteps. This "gatekeeping model" has left the artist, whether a writer, musician (who contends with record labels instead of publishers), cartoonist, and so on, in a bit of a void where no one can hear, read, or see what they have to say.

And then that new-fangled Internet blew in.

Ideas to Industry

Remember that saying someone's uncle said 300 years ago? "Ideas can change the world." I love ideas, and I enjoy few things as much as just sitting in a coffee shop sketching out my latest brainstorm.

Now comes the ugly truth: Ideas aren't worth a single red cent.

"What?!" you cry, "How can that be? Aren't we creative types driven by ideas? Aren't ideas our capital, our coalesced expressions that can be melted down and forged into art, fame, and riches? Aren't ideas worth more than all of the treasures sunk at the bottom of the Spanish Main?"

Well, no. Sorry.

Ideas are just that: ideas. Defined by dictionaries as "something, such as a thought or conception, that potentially or actually exists in the mind as a product of mental activity," they are the raw material with which we can eventually trade for real coin.

Ideas do not make money. *Processes* make money. This is a critical bit of knowledge that many creators ignore, and they ignore it at their financial peril. Your very best ideas aren't worth the napkins or envelopes they're scrawled on unless they are coupled with processes that generate money. Ideas, to be worth anything, have to be realized, refined, and packaged. Then, and only then, can they be traded for hard currency.

The industrial capitalists in the Renaissance understood this process very well. They put this sort of thing to practice by utilizing capital to amalgamate artisan work and thereby package and control all of the artisans in their employ. Prior to the introduction of industrial capitalism in the Renaissance, a master cobbler, for example, produced his wares, sold them to the consumer base, and collected the money, full stop. The cobbler was the final arbiter of quality, scheduling, and price. Some cobblers produced better shoes than others, whereas other cobblers were famous for their speed. The local market would pick from the cobblers that were nearby, although it was not uncommon for a single master to dominate a given area because of craftsmanship or prices.

Along came the money men, and with capital (defined as lots of liquid wealth that they can invest), they changed the face of the business of crafting. The capitalists employed the master cobblers and their apprentices, removing the onus of overhead from the masters' shoulders, which was clearly seen as a blessing by a great many of them. With a handful of master craftsmen and dozens of apprentices in their employ, the capitalists were able to standardize quality, price, and production. All of the money flowed into the coffers of the capitalists, and standard rates of pay flowed out to the employees, master and apprentice alike. In one swoop the capitalists amalgamated talent, took control of the product and its distribution, and funneled the flow of profits to their pockets. To be fair, keep in mind that the capitalists did take the not-insignificant risk of putting all of that wealth on the line. Business ventures are only a sure thing when you're breaking some kind of law or ethic.

Advance a few hundred years to the twentieth century and examine the landscape. In virtually every creative endeavor known to man, there is an industrial capital structure that in some way controls the money and distribution. Musicians have record labels; cartoonists and columnists have syndicates; painters and sculptors have galleries; filmmakers have studios; writers of every stripe have publishers (including the very fine publisher I'm working with to get this book to you). These capital structures effectively control the distribution of content to the masses, and their control has been absolute among themselves for well over a century.

It should be understood that this isn't an entirely bad thing! These structures do offer a service to the public, that of helping filter out (some of) the best content from the flotsam. Imagine if, say, a record label recorded and published every song submitted by any person (not just any musician) who took the time to drop off a demo tape: the resulting flood of music on the market would cause the consumer base to metaphorically gag on the influx of utter tripe that would make up 99 percent of the selections!

They also offer much-needed services to the artists. Publishers, for example, offer editing (to ensure standards of quality), printing and binding (they at least put up the capital for it), marketing (book shows, advertising, other promotion), and sales distribution (getting the books onto bookstore shelves). A writer who had to do all of this on his or her own would have to be rich, knowledgeable about book printing and book marketing, *and* would have to sell copies of his or her book into booksellers who have limited shelf space.

Something else publishers (or record labels, and so forth) do is keep an eye on the market. They usually have a pretty good idea of what will sell and what won't. They clearly won't take a risk on a manuscript that tells people how to grow azaleas in the arctic if there is no indication that Siberians or Alaskans or Northwest Territory residents are interested in the subject. The bigger publishers have entire departments devoted to collecting market data and analyzing consumer demands. Individual writers just don't have the resources to compete with this kind of business optimization.

This leads us to the conclusion that in the traditional marketspace, writers are best suited to writing. They can sequester themselves in whatever comfy room they prefer, and work their talent with words until a fine manuscript is wrought. The polished work is then handed over to a professional editor, who actually turns it into something marketable. And into the grinding gears of the publishing machine it goes, and at the end of the process that one manuscript has been transformed into 50,000 hard-cover books sitting on the shelves at Barnes & Noble. The books sell and the publisher pays the writer a (typically 5 percent to 15 percent) royalty based on the quantity sold. In some ways, it's a situation like the cobbler and the capitalist employers: the publisher has taken all of the financial risk, so they receive the lion's share of the revenue. However, the writer in the modern scenario is not an employee — he (or she) is a business partner, earning a percentage of the take. This structure ensures that the writer and the publisher are both motivated to see as many copies of the book are sold as possible, so the publisher will invest in marketing and the writer will endeavor to do his or her best work.

The birth of the Web has, of course, transformed the market as well as the business of publishing. The rulespace for delivering content to the masses is now shaped differently. None of this happened overnight.

I'm going throw the differences between the traditional and Web-based content rulespaces into sharp relief by explaining cartooning in terms of syndication and on-line delivery. Virtually everything I learned from my experiences with *User Friendly* can be applied to content of any sort on the Web, and how it compares to traditional methods of making money from selling content.

Syndicates: Businesses in Villains' Clothing

I mentioned earlier in this chapter that I had sent in cartoon submissions to six different syndicates, and like clockwork I received six rejection letters. After reading the previous section on industrial capitalism as it applies to content providers, you probably have an idea as to why I was rejected: my work wasn't good enough, or it simply didn't fit the needs of the market.

What a lot of people don't know is that the average cartoon syndicate receives more than 5,000 submissions per year, and they usually only have two open slots for new features. You read that correctly: two. Any new feature they bring on is a considerable gamble for them given how little room they have for developing, promoting, and selling new cartoon strips. It's much easier to just concentrate on the proven, established strips that are bringing in consistent revenue.

So, keeping in mind the realities of business risk and a generally conservative market (newspapers and their readers don't like to see much change in the comics section), it's amazing that there is *any* room for new features at all. Luckily for the creative types in the world, a demand for new cartoons, writing, music, and the like does exist. It just hasn't been particularly easy to see until the Web came along.

Before the Web, acceptance by a syndicate was really the only way anyone could make steady money as a cartoonist (note that I didn't say "make a living" — more on this later). They controlled the vertical, they controlled the horizontal, and they pretty much decided what cartoons would have a chance of seeing the light of day in the comics section. This kind of absolute control has its good and bad points, some of which have been previously discussed. The good points are obvious. The syndicates out of business necessity filter out the cruft that has no market, and they enforce a certain standard of quality. The bad points are just as obvious. The syndicates dictate to the entire consumer base which 20 comic features will become popular, out of a potential of thousands. Syndicates also make choices that will appeal the lowest common denominator in a consumer base, choosing to optimize their revenue over promoting high-quality work that may only appeal to a more educated or intelligent — and smaller — market segment.

This kind of control is known as *gatekeeping* (see Figure 1-1). The syndicates hold the keys to the gate through which content (traditionally) must pass through to reach the audience. Conversely, the audience (all 6 billion of us) has to buy a pass to step up to the gate and view the content on the other side.

FIGURE 1-1: Gatekeeping diagram

The astute observer will note that the syndicates take a piece of either money or control, or even both, whenever someone or something passes through that gate. As a cartoonist, I have to run the gauntlet and obtain explicit approval from a syndicate before I can bring my work to the gate. As consumer, my choices of content are entirely limited by what I can see on the other side of the gate. And when I pay to see that content, a piece of the toll ends up in the pocket of the syndicates controlling that gate.

Anyone with a passing understanding of the music industry will instantly see the parallel to the way record labels conduct business. In fact, the basic gatekeeping model is *the fundamental basis on which traditional companies that sell content do business*. It is this very control over the channels of distribution that empowers these companies. Creators want to create; consumers want to consume. The profit comes from bringing the two groups together and controlling the points at which they meet.

Syndicates make money by selling cartoon features they represent into newspapers and other publications. Once they've elected to bring a new cartoonist on board, they get the promotional machinery in motion and send out some of the new cartoonist's work samples to potential buyers. Alternatively, some (bigger) syndicates send out sales reps to the big newspaper conglomerates like Knight-Ridder. Appearing in a hundred papers at launch is a rare event indeed for a new feature. Fifty is considered very good, and a ten-paper launch isn't uncommon. Of course, much depends on the size of the papers: a cartoonist looking to earn a living would obviously rather be in ten papers with huge circulations than in 80 papers delivered to rural villages with tiny populations, and so would his or her syndicate.

The average payment from a newspaper for a daily feature seems to be around the $12 per week mark. A small paper might only pay $5 per week; a medium-sized city paper could afford $20 to $60 per week and the national or regional papers with monstrous circulations could offer a couple of hundred dollars per week.

For the sake of example, let's assume Our Hero the Cartoonist finds himself with a 50-paper launch (woo-hoo!). Assume $12 per week, and the total take would be around $2,400 per month. That's not a bad income just for drawing funny pictures every day.

But, the syndicate is going to want its piece of the pie. The most common (and really the best that can be hoped for) contracted split for a beginning creator is 50/50 — the syndicate takes its half for all of the promotion, selling, and development it helps you do. But that half-share is taken from the net proceeds, after deductions for things like promotional material and development costs. Some syndicates even try to sneak in an "Other costs, expenses or liabilities" clause, which gives them *carte blanche* to deduct whatever they please from gross revenues before calculating your half of the take. That's not particularly sporting, if you ask me.

So, now you're down to $1,200 per month assuming that you don't have any expenses deducted. Fifty papers don't seem to generate much cash. But this is normal! Cartooning, pretty much like every other type of content business out there, operates on a pyramid shaped like an isosceles triangle with a really big fat base (see Figure 1-2).

The bottom tier of the pyramid, the largest by far, is made up of the vast majority of syndicated cartoonists. They make considerably less than what you or I would consider a decent living. Some of them have day jobs, or they generate revenue by creating other features that they sell to publishers directly.

The tier just above this morass of the unwashed is the, er, washed cartoonists. There's not that many of them compared to the serfs below them. They pull in a decent sum, from the mid-five to low-six figure range. They're called "second tier" in the industry not because they're necessarily second-rate, but because they don't make the really big dollars.

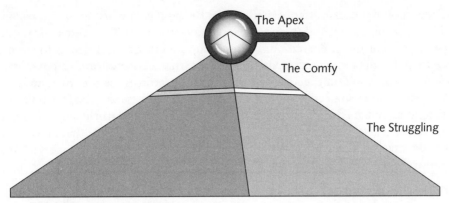

FIGURE 1-2: The creator's pyramid

The "top tier," the guys in the part of the pyramid you can barely see, are the superstars. They are the apex, the alpha, and the omega, and they are a license to print money as far as the syndicates are concerned. These are the Gary Larsons, Bill Wattersons, Jim Davises, Garry Trudeaus, and Berkely Breatheds of the cartooning industry. Millions of dollars fill the syndicate coffers thanks to the talents of these creators. Their creative properties become Saturday morning cartoons, branded merchandise, action figures, and breath mints. There are probably fewer than 20 of them at any given time.

Once again, even a barely conscious reader will note the similarities between cartoon syndication and the music business (and the film business, and column syndication, and art galleries, and and and. . .) — the system we have now for selling and distributing content was simply shaped by the demands of the free market economy and the difficulty of reaching wide audiences.

Enter the Web

The advent of the World Wide Web changed the equation. All of a sudden, the rules governing the distribution of content transformed. No longer did content creators have to approach a syndicate, record label, or other business with their work. In the blink of an eye, creators had a direct line to millions of consumers, and the cost to deliver content to this international audience is a tiny fraction of the traditional methods of distribution. The really pathetic part of it all was that the creative class mostly just blinked at this new way of getting our work out there. We just didn't really know what to do or how to take advantage of this newfound power.

The response was, admittedly, predictable. Remember the history of craftsman-ship and capitalism? And the psychology of creative people? Creative people are unquestionably talented, but our deep passion for our art often seems to leave lit-tle room for the kind of pragmatic perspective that a business expert possesses. We're so caught up in the idea that the obvious processes seem to melt away from our view. Rather than cope with the mundane (but necessary) tasks involved in generating dollars from our work, we'd rather shut out the world and just focus on what we love. The creative class is largely made up of people that are a bit like mildly retarded kids with savant abilities, and we're just as easy to take advantage of if we're not aware and guarded.

But eventually things turned around a bit for content on the Web. The first step was getting the content up there, and I did just that in November of 1997 after I had scrawled a half-dozen or so cartoons to pass around the office. I was a partner working at a small boutique Internet service provider (ISP), and cartooning became a way for me to blow off some stress. The senior partner suggested that I put the few cartoons I had done up on the Web — which I initially resisted! Like so many creative people, my first thought was, "Who'd want to read them?" And like so many people with business smarts, the senior partner very gently cajoled me into giving it a go.

By April of 1998, the first Web site for *User Friendly* was generating a mediocre 34,000 page impressions a month. However, my audience had expanded from the original dozen or so friends and acquaintances to several hundred, and that's sev-eral hundred strangers that I had never met before in my life. Word of mouth was the method of marketing, one that I hadn't counted on or understood. The Web had let me completely sidestep the gate being kept by the comic syndicates.

Thirty-four thousand pages doesn't seem like much right now, but at the time I was thrilled. My work was being read and enjoyed! I was receiving supportive, appreciative e-mails from Marie in South Carolina and Tuomo in Helsinki! I had at least one fan in a country that spoke English as a second language!

The thrill soon gave way to incredulity. By June of 1998, I was up to a quarter of a million page views per month. December 1998 saw nearly 5 million page views. And guess what — no syndicate!

The Web caused a significant ripple to pass through the traditional business of content provision. The gate that was so carefully guarded by the myriad gatekeep-ers was suddenly bypassed, and they had absolutely no control over the Internet. After a few years, it was crystal clear that they had to adapt to and embrace the new technology, or see their revenue erode over time.

There were several moments of vindication yet to come, but seeing *User Friendly's* popularity take off on a hockey-stick curve was the first one that caused me to realize that the world of content had really changed. At the time I wasn't precisely overflowing with solutions for generating money from my work; I was too busy reveling in the fact that as an unknown artist I could get my content out to the world without the permission or aid of the gatekeepers.

That incredulity soon turned to fear. I was racking up some serious bandwidth bills and had no way to really pay for them. I sought the advice of my business partners (one of whom still works with me at *User Friendly*) and they both felt this was an opportunity rather than a problem.

It seemed odd to me at the time that I was having such trouble with seeing the processes that needed to be put into place to build revenue from my work. I had the better part of a decade in experience as a creative director and business unit manager. I was pretty good at turning production teams into profitable work centers. What I failed to realize was that an entirely new business model wasn't needed to make a content play on the Web a financial success. What we needed to do was apply a modified version of proven business processes, but I just didn't see that. I was so convinced that because the Web was new, only new models would work. This is where the high-altitude understanding of business processes, something my partners had in spades and I had in spoonfuls, was needed.

As usual, the process people were correct. I was so focused on my cartooning that I couldn't see the forest for the great big hole right in front of me. All I had to do was step over it and I'd be under a canopy of money.

chapter

The Advertising Game

As a private person, I have a passion for landscape, and I have never seen one improved by a billboard.

— David Ogilvy of Ogilvy & Mather

Advertising has been with us since the first day someone created something they wanted to sell or barter, be it a service or a product. It is, at its core, simply the practice of informing a potential buyer of the existence of something he or she might want to purchase. Once the element of competition was added, advertising evolved into the practice of singing the praises of something someone might want to buy.

The very first newspaper advertisement was placed in 1704, in the *Boston News-Letter*. It was an announcement seeking a buyer for an estate in Long Island. In 1742, Benjamin Franklin's *General Magazine* printed the very first American magazine ads. Just a bit over a century later, the first dedicated advertising agency was opened in Philadelphia by Volner Palmer (yes, *that* Palmer). From a twentieth-century point of view, I'm surprised it took that long.

By the 1870s, advertising had developed into quite a lucrative and calculated art. This hasn't changed in more than a hundred years, but the competition is certainly much fiercer and more sophisticated. The audience is more sophisticated as well, but that comes from being inundated by advertising as opposed to any sort of evolution of tastes or character.

We are, as a culture, overwhelmed with ambivalence when it comes to advertising. On the one hand we despise it and its intrusions. You almost can't turn anywhere without seeing someone's marketing message or call to action blaring in your face. On the other hand, we enjoy witty or moving ads, ones that either have some artistry behind them or that appeal to our baser instincts. So, while we all complain about how advertising has destroyed our cultural landscape, we sit and watch the Super Bowl mostly to catch the ads that come on at halftime. There isn't a single North American adult of either gender who hasn't heard of *Victoria's Secret*. We argue over whether Pepsi or Coke tastes better, and quite frankly they're both pretty similar. Sprite and 7-Up? What about domain providers? Is GoDaddy really the best place to by a dot com name, or do we just like their spokesmodel with the centerfold body? What does all of this tell us?

It tells us that advertising works. The fact that it is such a pervasive cultural force today tells us that it works really well, or at least well enough to sustain itself. There can be no denying that despite the litany of things we hate about advertising, we still remain under its thrall.

Human psychology has become an important supporting field in advertising. We know quite a bit about the way people read and absorb information. Many television commercials in Japan are played twice, right after each other, because it was learned that there is greater retention of information when this happens. We've studied what sentence structures are most impactful and what layouts have the greatest effect. Colors are assigned different values of appeal for specific moods. We've learned that it's easy to fool a television viewer's sense of discrimination and take advantage of this weakness. In commercials that sell products that make you more attractive, most people don't notice that the model in the "before" shot looks depressed (and is often shot in black-and-white), and the "after" shot has the model smiling brilliantly. All we notice is that the model in the "after" shot looks several orders of magnitude more attractive, and this sends a message to our ego: buy this product and you'll look that much better! (See Figure 2-1.)

ADVERTISMENT TRANSLATION:
"IF YOU BUY THIS FANCY BRA,
YOUR WIFE WILL LOOK LIKE
THIS MODEL."

FIGURE 2-1: Advertisement translation

The Players

There are four major players in any given advertising effort: the client, the ad agency, the ad network or sales force, and the media channel (or publisher). All four work together to get an advertising campaign from concept to delivery, and then perform analysis of the campaign after the delivery. As mentioned before, advertising is a calculated art, this fact being clearest when all of the numbers are crunched during and especially after a campaign.

The Client

These are the people with all of the money, whether it's a little or a lot. They have a product or service that they want potential customers to know about. Further, they want their potential customers to think favorably about their product or service. This is the ultimate goal of any marketing strategy, and many millions of dollars have been spent in the attempt.

Clients can be sophisticated marketers, but they still often rely on advertising agencies to do the really heavy lifting. The larger the company, the greater the chance that they'll be involved with an advertising agency, and the company's vice president of marketing will be the client's representative. Companies with huge marketing departments still go to advertising agencies, because the agencies specialize in areas that in-house marketing departments generally do not. Large portions of in-house marketing departments are devoted to measuring the success of ad campaigns and studying the market and the forces within those markets with an eye toward finding the best way to inject their product into consumer awareness.

In your role as a publisher, the odds are not high that you'll be dealing directly with clients. However, the more popular your site is, the greater the chance that a client will contact you directly. This is because sites with lots of traffic represent a major channel into a specific audience all on its own, and those sites will appear on a potential client's radar. Also, some clients — regardless of the size of the company they represent — would rather have a direct hand in the creative content of the campaign. This may be because it'll save them money, or because they enjoy the greater control (and, therefore, the greater risk and reward) involved.

When you deal with a client on your own, you'll have to discuss the division of the other roles: is the client responsible for the advertising creative or are you? Will the client be serving ads from its own server and redirecting through yours, or are you taking on and managing the whole thing? Who does the post-campaign analysis? What are the terms of the contract (remembering that this is a client who may or may not be a sophisticated media channel buyer, and so on)?

If the preceding paragraph confused you or filled you with dread, relax. All will be revealed as you march through this book. All you need to know now is that when you're dealing with a client, you may make more money, but you'll also probably deal with headaches that are an order of magnitude greater than if you dealt with an ad agency or ad network.

For most site owners, clients will be faceless, shadowy creatures drawn from the pages of myth and legend. At most, you'll know who is advertising what product. Their banner ads will be run on your site and eventually you'll be paid the agreed-upon sum for doing so. Unless you have people helping you, or you have more time in the day than you know what to do with, this is probably the best situation to be in.

Don't misunderstand me; clients aren't some kind of necessary evil. They are nec-essary, because without them there'd be no money for advertising and, therefore, no ad dollars will land in your pocket, but they're not evil. They're just people who want to make sure that they're getting the most they can from their marketing dollars. If you were in their position, I'd wager you'd behave the same way.

The Advertising Agency

Three distinct kinds of agencies serve the advertising industry: boutique agencies, media agencies, and full-service agencies. The odds are you'll only ever deal with the last one, but let's cover them all just for the sake of perspective.

A *boutique agency* is a (typically) small service organization that specializes in the creative portion of the advertising process, which includes art, photography, copy-writing, concepts, and bringing together an overarching advertising message. Boutique agencies do not, as a rule, offer other advertising services such as media planning or buying.

Media agencies are organizations that focus on media planning, media research, and media buying, effectively performing every advertising function that a bou-tique agency does not. Media agencies were once known as "buying services," which was a less-than-accurate title given the fact that they also performed media planning and research functions.

A *full-service agency* (also simply referred to by default as an "ad agency") is a ser-vice organization that creates advertising messages on behalf of its clients and selectively places those messages in various media channels. Also, agencies per-form a multitude of other advertising functions, including business or market research, media planning, developing the ad creative that goes into the entire range of media channels, and overseeing the production of (or actually producing) ad spots for television and radio.

The part that should mostly concern you as a publisher is the placement of advertising. Ad agencies spend a significant percentage of their operating hours researching and analyzing what, how, when, and where to place their clients' advertising. To earn their business, you need to make your content site an appeal-ing place to put advertising and, of course, for them to put their clients' money in your bank account.

Advertising agencies make their money by being "awarded accounts" — a client signs a contract with them that commits their advertising budget for a product or service to that agency. The agency typically receives a commission and fees for every ad placement in a media channel. A $1 million placement could earn an agency upwards of 20 percent, which motivates them to get advertising campaigns up and running. Campaigns that fail badly (or even moderately) usually spell the end of any given account, so the money can't be spent indiscriminately.

Before a prudent advertising agency makes a decision to place a campaign in a specific media channel, it conducts market research and examines the myriad factors that can impact the success of advertising in that channel. If the results of that research are favorable (read: risk is minimized), the agency will issue what is known as an Advertising RFP or "Request for Proposal." This is a document that is given by media buyers to media sellers (publishers of whatever stripe) asking for a proposal to advertise within their medium. The buyer will typically detail the various objectives and parameters such as timing, the need for added value (industry nomenclature for "unique, useful freebies that will help the campaign"), and creative units (the kinds of ads to be used) that are planned. A typical advertising RFP summary might look like Figure 2-2.

In short, the advertising agency is requesting Web advertising packages from publishers that have a reach into the desktop developer audience. Its goal is to attract "Microsoft-friendly" developers (coders who make a living writing application code for Windows) and "technology decision-makers" (IT managers who have planning and implementation authority).

The kicker is always the way that the campaign is measured, known as the "metrics." The agency is requiring a cost ceiling of $100 per registrant, which means that for every $100 of advertising they buy from a publisher, there must be at least one registrant to the conference. For a publisher to collect fully on a (for example) $40,000 buy, at least 400 people must register for the conference from that publisher's audience. If during the campaign that metric is violated, the agency will pull the campaign.

A responding proposal might look like Figure 2-3.

After the deadline, the agency reviews all of the proposals that were submitted and selects one (or more, depending on its strategy and budget) and does what is known in the industry as "makes a buy." A contract is negotiated, signed, and the advertising campaign begins.

Request for Proposal (Advertising)

Proposal Due Date: 3/29/05

Campaign Start Date: 6/13/05

Campaign End Date: 8/31/05

About the Client:

Microsoft is looking to reach developers through multiple online media placements and drive registrations for the Professional Developers Conference (PDC) to be held in September 2005. The PDC is a technology conference held specifically for developers who want to gain a deeper understanding and get an early glimpse into the Microsoft vision of the next wave of the platform. It will be Microsoft's mission to "convince desktop software developers that the Microsoft Longhorn technologies can make their lives easier and pay off for the users of their software."

About the Campaign:

Microsoft is looking to utilize contextually relevant online media vehicles to drive registrations for the PDC event in September.

Points of Interest:

- Flight: 6/13/05 – 8/31/05
- Targeted to Microsoft friendly (MSDN) Professional Developers (Primary) and Technology Decision Makers (Secondary)

Campaign Objective:

The primary goal is to **drive registrants to the PDC event in September** at a cost per registration below $100.

Performance Metrics:

- Online registrations
- Increase awareness of the PDC event within the target audience and encourage participation
- Increase awareness of Microsoft products: Visual Studio 2005, Yukon and Longhorn

Budget:

Please submit proposals between $15,000 and $25,000 (per month). Only reasonable rates will be considered.

Contact:

D. Lane, 212-555-4242, dlane@agency.com

FIGURE 2-2: Sample RFP summary

Advertising proposal for Microsoft PDC Conference

Objectives

- Drive registrations to the PDC event.
- Increase awareness of PDC and generate interest in both gaining an early glimpse and a deeper understanding of Microsoft's vision of the platforms next wave.
- Help convince desktop software developers that Microsoft Longhorn technologies can make their lives easier and pay off the users of their software.

Target Audience
Professional Developers (Primary) and Technology Decision Makers (Secondary)

Media Partner: TechSite.Com

TechSite.Com is all about information technology and the people who work within the sector every day.

Traffic:
- Over 500,000 Unique Visitors per month
- Over 8,000,000 impressions per month
- 6.30 sessions per visitor per month---more than most IT centric need-to-visit sites.
- 52% spend 5 or more hours per month at TechSite.Com

Audience:

- 67% are in core IT Occupations (39% Developers – Primary Target Audience)
- 71% recommend hardware/software purchases (Secondary Target Audience)
- The top 40 proxy sites hitting TechSite.Com originate from major corporations or institutions

Advertisers:
Main advertisers include IBM, HP, Apple and Orion.

Strategy:

1) Educate developers of the benefits of Microsoft Longhorn technologies.
2) Educate developers and Microsoft about what users think of respective Microsoft Products (Visual Studio 2005, Yukon and Longhorn.) via custom polls.
3) Parlay developer's feelings for TechSite.Com into halo effect for Microsoft. Similar to celebrity spokespeople.

Content integration section, in which Microsoft's Longhorn Development Center will reside for all 3 Months of the push and will be prominently featured in the site's navigation bar/links.

Media Plan:

Ad Unit	Placement	CPM	Total Imps.	Cost (Net)
336x280	Homepage	$4	750,000	$3,000
336x280	ROS	$3	250,000	$750
728 x 90	Homepage	$2	200,000	$400
728 x 90	ROS	$1	200,000	$200
120 x 600	Homepage	$2	200,000	$400
120 x 600	ROS	$1	200,000	$200

Total Media Cost: $4,950

Total Media Impressions: 3,800,000

Net Media CPM: $1.30

Sales Contact – Robert Loblaw

Tel: (604) 555-4242 Fax: (604) 555-4343 Email: (rlob@techsite.com)

FIGURE 2-3: Responding proposal

The Ad Network and the Sales Force

These are the people that you will often find working between and with an ad agency (or client *sans* agency) and a publisher. As a site owner, it is this group that you will be dealing with the vast majority of the time. Ad networks include Doubleclick, 24/7 Real Media, Clickhouse, Google's AdSense, Rydium, and so on.

Ad networks go around aggregating pageviews from Web sites and selling them to ad agencies and/or clients. For example, a network may have commitments with 20 Web sites, each serving a million pages a month. The network then sends proposals and makes sales calls to ad agencies, who buy blocks of impressions from the network. The network sends the ads to the Web sites, the ads are served, and the network collects the money from the agencies. A commission is taken from the fees collected and the site owners get the rest of the money.

This is the process in a nutshell. Ad networks effectively take the business of selling advertising out of the hands of the site owners. Unless you're particularly good at selling ads, or you have more hours in a day than you know what to do with, an ad network is really a godsend.

Dedicated *sales forces* are much like ad networks but are a little more exclusive. Sales forces sign commitments with Web sites that have significant traffic (say, in excess of 5 million pageviews per month) and a good handle on their audience profile. Rather than selling a general campaign of, say, 5 million MasterCard banners across ten smaller Web sites, a dedicated sales force will sell campaigns specifically targeted to the sites they represent. Sales forces also don't do any ad serving themselves; they just pass on the creative to the site owner, which means if you want to avail yourself of the benefits of working with a sales force, you'll need to run your own ad server.

For example, UserFriendly.org (UF) has a large (well over a million readers) audience, most of whom are technologists or work in information technology. If our dedicated sales force spots a media request for a technology-centric audience, they'll write a proposal involving UF as the media channel and submit it on my behalf. If the agency makes the buy, UF works with the sales force to keep the agency happy by managing the campaign. The sales force collects the payment and sends it to UF after subtracting their commission.

The number of ad networks you'll want to join will be dictated by a few factors. Obviously the most important one is performance. Would you rather work with one or two ad networks that consistently get you $3 CPMs or ten ad networks who get you $.10 CPMs? (What this means is $3 for every 1,000 banners served or 10 cents for every 1,000 banners served.) Some ad networks specialize in, for example, lifestyle advertising such as mass consumer product companies (Old Navy, MasterCard,

Pepsi, and so on), whereas others may specialize in narrow verticals, selling advertising space to companies that produce mining software, woodworking tools, model-specific synthesizer chips, and the like. You'll probably want a small mix, and definitely more than just one ad network, because not every ad network can sell every ad impression you have available, and a page with a blank instead of an ad is a wasted opportunity to make revenue.

If you go with a dedicated sales force, I'd find one that really understands what your site and audience are about and stick with them. Bolster that with one or more ad networks so that you have lower-profit, but more consistent dollars coming in during those months that your sales force doesn't manage to sell targeted campaigns on your site. Above all, think really hard before you sign an exclusive with anyone — you could be cutting yourself off from other revenue streams if you do that, with little recourse. If you do sign an exclusive, be absolutely firm on getting some kind of performance guarantee. Most networks won't agree to the latter, which also has the side effect of you not signing an exclusive with anyone. That's a win for you as far as I'm concerned.

A secondary caveat: Be sure to watch how you allocate your ad inventory. Handing off large pieces of your inventory to the backfilling ad networks can demolish your ad rates once word gets out that you're handing out a million impressions for $200 through the networks. Any dedicated sales force is going to be frustrated if you keep undercutting them, so be sure to give them priority and agree on a strategy with them. It doesn't do them or you any good if an ad network sells a million ads on your site to Cisco for a $0.10 CPM while your sales force is pitching a media package to the same customer that would net you 50 times that.

The Media Channel

Millions of media channels are available to advertisers, and if you own a content site, you're one of them. A *media channel* is focal point where content is delivered via a particular medium, be it television, radio, print, or the Web. Example media channels would be *The New York Times*, 96.9 JackFM, CBS, *Cosmopolitan*, any university newspaper, `arstechnica.com`, `cnet.com`, and so forth. All of these entities are, in one way or another, venues for content that attracts a certain readership. A common synonym is "publisher," although that's more accurate for the Web and print than radio or television.

Most of the large media channels have their own dedicated sales forces marketing and selling "advertising opportunities" (a collective term for space in print publications, pageviews on the Web, and airtime on television, radio, and podcasts) to agencies and clients. Unless you're sitting on a whole lot of capital, I expect you'll be signing on with an ad network or three, rather than selling on your own. However, just because you sign on to a network, it doesn't mean you should completely take yourself out of the picture.

Every time a network or sales force secures a campaign, they'll end up taking roughly half of the revenue earned. Money from media buys that you land yourself will naturally go entirely to you, and if you're big enough, agencies and clients will contact you directly. But where do you draw the line?

Here's a rule of thumb that has worked well for me at UF: If the agency or client requires an involved written proposal, or if the dollar figure involved is 10 percent or more of my annual revenues, I'll hand the contact off to the professionals at the sales force. Remember that these guys are good at what they do or they won't be in business for long. Yes, you're giving up around half of the potential dollars, but would you rather a 90 percent chance at earning 50 percent of $10,000 or a 10 percent chance at earning 100 percent of $10,000? You don't need to understand risk calculations to see how the first choice is vastly better. You're in this to make money, so don't let egotistical (or greedy!) "I can do it all myself" thinking get in the way of smart business decisions.

Demographics

Demography measures the characteristics of population segments, particularly when used to identify consumer markets. Demographic factors most often measured in media planning and buying include gender, age, household income, education levels, number of employees at workplace, workplace revenue, and the respondent's degree of influence in the process of purchasing products and services.

The demographics of the audience that visits your site is, without question, the most valuable data that you can possess when dealing with advertisers. Advertisers (or their agencies) are more than willing to drop a bag full of coin in your lap if you can put them in front of the right people, and the way you can convince them that you do indeed have the audience they want is by showing them the data that proves it.

Conducting a Survey

Surveying is big business today. Market research depends on solid demographic data in the same way that humans depend on oxygen. Without it, market researchers would have nothing to work from or on, and advertisers would be skittish about paying money for getting their product or service in front of an unqualified audience. Imagine if you could place an ad to sell your boat, but the ad would be shown to people from the general population, including people who aren't even remotely interested in boating. Would you be inclined to pay much for that kind of exposure? What if you had to pay twice as much, but for that your ad would be run in *Boating Magazine*? The choice is a no-brainer.

Clearly, demographic data is highly valuable. There are some truly enormous corporations whose sole business is the collection and analysis (and ultimately the sale) of demographic and market data (Ipsos-Reid and Gallup come to mind). These companies have refined surveying to something that approaches scientific rigor, which is critical because data that isn't accurate is worthless to advertisers.

You have two options when it comes to collecting demographic data: you can contract a company to do it, or you can do it yourself. The former choice has an obvious downside: it costs money, potentially lots of money. The upside is that you don't need to worry about collecting and sorting the data, and you will have the benefit of third-party validation of your data. The latter choice costs you little (if any) money, but the downside is that you have to do all of the hard work of designing and deploying the survey. You'll also have to verify and sort the data collected in hopes of making some sense of it all.

I'll make the assumption that you'll be taking the second route, since involving a company such as Ipsos-Reid in your survey will run you five figures just to get started. Doing most or all of it yourself isn't as difficult as it may sound, especially if you're only running a survey to collect information about your audience. But you do need to understand what steps are taken in conducting a survey to ensure that it is "scientifically" accurate.

A couple of online survey outfits that are more affordable to the independent creator are surveycompany.com and www.nooro.com. Neither is particularly inexpensive, but they don't usually command rates in the five-figure range either. When you're pulling in an audience of more than 100,000, it's time to spend money with a reputable survey firm that can guide you through the survey process and return useful money-making information to you.

What a Survey Is Not

Let's debunk a few things about surveys right off the cuff. A poll you find on a Web site is not a survey, except in the broadest meaning of the term (see Figure 2-4). Surveys are not just a collection of questions and some tallying at the end. Surveys are not qualitative; that is, they are meant to collect information that can't be quantified. Finally, surveys are never flawless. You will always have some inaccuracy in your results, but certain levels are acceptable for market research purposes.

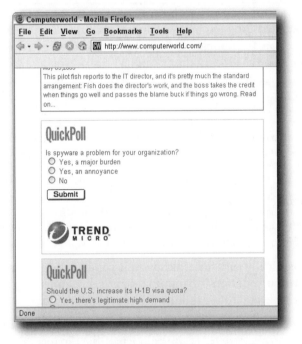

FIGURE 2-4: A Web poll is not a survey!

There is no simple five-step rote procedure I know of for designing surveys. When you're designing for a new audience or a new objective, it's best just to start from scratch and think about what you're trying to achieve. In our case, we're trying to come up with a survey that provides us with demographic information that we can use to attract advertisers.

Questions, Answers, and Legerdemain

One of the most important objectives in conducting surveys is minimizing bias. If you consider the number of human factors involved in a survey, it's really quite astonishing that we're able to derive much usable data at all. For example, you shouldn't just leave your survey up in a section of your Web site for anyone to take, because then you introduce the bias of *self-selection*. This refers to the kind of personality that enjoys filling out surveys, or at least enjoys it more than other personalities. To avoid this bias, your survey should be made available to your audience randomly.

Perhaps the most difficult bias to minimize is the one intrinsic to the questions themselves. Asking "do you like filling in questionnaires?" is so hopelessly biased that the results for that question are completely useless. The wording of a question is critical as well. "What do you eat for breakfast?" and "What do you like to eat for breakfast?" are two subtly, yet decidedly different questions. Remember that you will only get the answers to the questions you ask, and even then there will be some sampling errors and bias creeping in.

Now that you're aware of the minefield, let's consider the data points that you should be collecting. These are data that all ad agencies and ad networks are interested in:

- *Gender* — Male or female, and yes it matters.

- *Age* — Age brackets are usually sufficient. A very common breakdown is Under 18, 18 to 25, 26 to 35, 36 to 45, 46 to 65, 66 and up.

- *Location* — Country is usually sufficient, although if you have an audience that is almost entirely in one nation (if you run a political commentary site, for example) it would be useful to break it down by region or state.

- *Occupation* — Occupational sectors are usually fine: Management, Government, Education, Manufacturing, Creative, Technical, Scientific, Finance, Retail, Wholesale, Communications, and so on.

- *Annual Income* — Brackets again are acceptable. Up to $20K, $21K to $40K, $41K to $60K, $61K to $80K, $81K to $100K, $101K and above.

- *Amount of time spent on line per day* — Bracketed. Up to 1 hour, 1 to 2 hours, 2 to 4 hours, 4 to 8 hours, more than 8 hours.

- *Personal Spending (Annual)* — Depending on the content you provide, adjust this data point as appropriate. UF is dominated by a technologist audience, so "Personal Tech Spending" data is what we collect.

- *Role in Purchasing for Workplace* — This data point is of great interest to vendors (who are the advertisers!) that supply businesses. The most commonly accepted responses are: None, Influence, Recommend, Decision-maker.

- *Company Size (Employees)* — Don't assume that having an audience made up largely of small company employees is a bad thing. Often, that means the audience is full of Recommenders or Decision-makers. Of course, having the CEOs of major banks visiting your site daily would be a real coup. Bracket the company sizes as well: up to 50, 51 to 100, 101 to 250, 251 to 500, 501 to 1000, 1001 to 10,000, and 10,001 and up.

- *Company Annual Revenues* — Advertisers like to know what kind of money (which could become theirs) sits behind your audience. Under $1 million, $1 million to $10 million, $11 million to $100 million, $101 million to $500 million, over $500 million.

- *Company Spending (Annual)* — This data point needs to be customized just like the personal spending one. Since UF mostly attracts technology companies for advertising, the data point is "Company Tech Spending (Annual)."

Those points are the ones you should be collecting at a minimum. However, don't overdo your survey with questions. You need to hold a person's interest long enough for them to finish the questionnaire, otherwise any data they provide will never get to you.

An absolute upper limit for the time needed to fill out a survey seems to be 20 minutes, but for collecting data about your audience I'd recommend keeping it to five minutes or less — unless you're offering them some kind of reward that you know they'll want for completing the survey.

Now that you have a list of data points you have to collect, you need to write out your questions. In all of the ones listed here, you'll note that they're what are called "closed-end questions." In other words, they're questions with definitive answers that you have provided as a multiple-choice selection. These are far more preferable in a scientific survey, because open-ended questions tend to be qualitative and are very difficult to quantify.

When you write out your questions be sure that you trim them down to be as concise as possible. Don't add modifiers or anything that might confuse the reader. The writing should be business-like and formal.

When you write the multiple-choice answers to go with the questions, be particularly careful that there are no overlaps or significant gaps. For example, when asking for someone's age, ensure that the age brackets don't run "up to 18, 18–25. . ." because an 18-year-old could select either one and be answering truthfully. When asking about annual income, " . . .$21K to $30K, $31K to $40K. . ." is sufficient, even if there's a gap between $30K and $31K — the key is that the gap is not significant, and most respondents will subconsciously round off to one or the other as appropriate.

One other caveat about questions and answers: If you are not absolutely certain that you have included every possible valid answer for a question, add the answer "other." When asking someone for their occupation, if your list isn't complete, part of the time the respondent will simply pick what is closest and the rest of the time the respondent will just drop the survey. You don't want either of these results! Do your research carefully and have friends look the questions over for you with fresh eyes. Once you deploy a survey, that's it — if you find a serious flaw in the questioning after the fact, all of the data collected up until that point is suspect and has to be discarded. The obvious rule here is to be rigorous in reviewing your questions before deploying the survey. Rigor is required to ensure that the questions and answers are worded correctly, and that you're asking the correct questions.

Lastly, when you design a survey, don't include questions asking for personally identifiable information (such as names, Social Security numbers, and so on). You'll turn off such a large percentage of your potential survey pool that you'll never collect a large enough sample. Some people may think you're phishing, which will do your reputation little good.

Speaking of samples, the number that seems to make most people in media buying happy is a bit over a thousand. You don't need to have a sample much larger than that to have data that is considered valuable.

There is a plethora of surveying software available on the Web. Places you can start looking include SurveyGold, WebSurveyor, and KeySurvey. Your choices are legion, and every week more survey packages become available, so be sure to do a lot of comparison shopping.

Something else you should be aware of is third-party verification of your data. If you can afford to have a third party run your survey for you (and I mean a reputable surveying firm), it's often worth the money, but generally only if you have a large number of pageviews, say in excess of a couple of million a month. It's a nice thing to be able to add a "Verified by $THIRDPARTY" cutline to your demographics, and media buyers notice this. On the other hand, many of the larger Web sites have done just fine without this, and there's a good reason for it.

You might be thinking, "What's to stop me from falsifying my data and making me look amazingly attractive to advertisers?" There are two obstacles. One, if the campaign doesn't perform as a media buyer expects it should, they'll pull the campaign and you get little or no money. And two (this is the most critical obstacle), media buyers talk among themselves. If word gets out that your demographics don't seem to jibe with your site's performance, you could get yourself blackballed.

Figure 2-5 shows a sample survey.

Annual Audience Survey

The following is a survey that collects information about our audience, and you have been randomly chosen to participate. As this information is crucial in our efforts to sell advertising and keep this site open and free, we would greatly appreciate your co-operation. The survey should only take about five minutes of your time. If you would rather not do so, click here to be taken back to the main page.

What is your gender?
Male
Female

What is your age?
Under 18
18 to 25
26 to 35
36 to 45
46 to 65
66 and up

What is the highest level of education you have completed?
Did not complete High School
High School
Some Post-Secondary
Vocational or Technical College
Baccalaureate Degree
Masters Degree
Doctorate
Post-Doctorate

What is your own yearly income?
Under to $20,000
$20,000 to $35,000
$36,000 to $50,000
$51,000 to $75,000
$76,000 to $100,000
Over $100,000

What is your combined household income?
Under to $30,000
$30,000 to $60,000
$61,000 to $90,000
$91,000 to $120,000
$121,000 to $150,000
Over $1510,000

What is your annual spending on technology for personal use?
Under $500
$500 to $1000
$1001 to $2500
$2501 to $5000
Over $5000

What is your occupational sector?
Manufacturing
Military
Government
Creative
Hospitality & Tourism
Agriculture
Health
Retail
Sales/Marketing/Promotion
Trades
Shipping/Distribution
Information Technology
Student
Retired
Unemployed

How many employees do you have at your workplace?
Under 10
10 to 50
51 to 100
101 to 500
501 to 1000
1001 to 5000
Over 5000

What are your workplace's estimated annual revenues?
Under $100,000
$100,000 to $1 million
$2 million to $5 million
$6 million to $25 million
$26 million to $100 million
$101 million to $500 million
$501 million to $1 billion
Over $1 billion

What is your workplace's annual technology budget?
Under $10,000
$10,000 to $50,000
$50,001 to $100,000
$100,001 to $500,000
$500,001 to $1 million
$2 million to $5 million
$6 million to $25 million
Over $25 million

What is your role in company technology purchases?
No role
Influencer
Recommender
Decision-maker

Thank you for participating in our annual audience profile survey. None of the data we collect is personally identifiable and will only be used in aggregate.

FIGURE 2-5: Sample survey

I Have the Data. . . Now What?

Having a beer is a good start. You're still not done with the survey. Now that you have the data, you need to transform it into something useful.

That something is what is known as a *media kit*. This is promotional material about your site that explains the virtues of advertising there, showcases your audience data, and describes advertising options and costs. This isn't something you need to have printed; UF has been using digital media kits (a la Adobe Acrobat) for years now, and they're more than sufficient. Besides, the vast majority of media kit requests you get will be via e-mail.

Begin doing a percentage breakdown of all of your data. If you collected 2,000 valid responses — an invalid survey response is one that wasn't completed, or was spoiled in some way, and should be discarded — and 600 of them replied "Female" to your Gender question, you know that 30 percent of your audience is female and 70 percent is male.

When calculating percentages, it's perfectly acceptable to round to the nearest tenth of a percent, or even full percentage point. Whatever rounding or clustering you do, be sure to keep your original data backed up in a safe place in case a media agency asks for more specific data.

Once you've done all of the percentages, review your data and consider if clustering some of the data points would be useful. Do your media buyers really care how many students and retirees are in your audience? If not, perhaps clustering them together with Unemployed would be more expedient. If you think most of your advertisers will be very large product firms, they may not be interested in the companies with fewer than 50 employees, so clustering the Under 10 Employees and 10 to 50 Employees data points would also be smart.

The idea here is to only tell the absolute truth with your data, but to also put your demographics in the best possible light for your advertisers. Never lie, but also keep foremost in your mind that your media kit is a promotional tool for your site and advertising space.

The Media Kit

Your data has been clustered and written out and you're ready to build your media kit. I highly recommend using some kind of layout program such as InDesign, Quark XPress, or Pagemaker, and rendering PDFs from whichever one you use. You will need three sections at minimum, but don't overdo your kit. Media buyers don't have a lot of time to read, and they really just want to get to the guts of your offering. If you can keep it down to five or fewer pages, you're doing fine.

The three fundamental sections in an online media kit are the Introduction (or "brag sheet"), the Demographics, and the Offer (see Figure 2-6). The Introduction is all about explaining your site's mandate and, where possible, a place to highlight flattering quotes, reviews, and other commentary that makes it look attractive as an advertising venue. A good rule of thumb is to keep the number of words down to 500 or less in this section — it needs to be eye-catching and inspiring, not a long, droning testament to your site's success.

The Demographics section is exactly what it sounds like. This is where you'll be providing data about your audience, and the media buyers will be spending a fair amount of time on this page. Again, keep it concise and clear, and make sure the section is easy to read.

The Offer section is where you detail what you can offer a media buyer (how many ad impressions and of what shapes and sizes, for example). If you have special deals or campaign bundles, this is where you describe them. It's also a good idea to mention that you can do custom campaigns to suit. A lot of media buyers (particularly ones who represent large buys) won't be interested in your offers, but whether or not you can accommodate their campaign specifics. This is also where you can place your rates (thus the Offer section also doubles as your rate card) for your banner ads, but I recommend against this. Rather than set prices that most people will want to negotiate anyway, it's smarter to just keep the prices off, giving you the option to come up with a number tailored to each request.

If you're someone with a site that has fairly hefty traffic, you might also want to add a campaign value restriction to your Offer section. For UF, I won't consider any campaigns that are worth less than $500. As much as I'd love to be able to take small campaigns worth $20 or $50 bucks each, if I did that I'd be forever managing campaigns and would have little time left for cartooning and writing!

It's a very good idea to check out your competition's media kits, and other media kits in general. They'll give you ideas with regard to formatting and the kind of information you should be including in your own kit. Any of the top three search engines reveals a plethora of media kits available for examination online.

Who you show your media kit is up to you, but I do recommend that you leave it offline and only e-mail it to people who specifically ask for it or require the demographics data. Media kits are great for passing on information quickly, but the most important part of the selling process is engaging the customer in a dialogue. You'll find more success responding to a "May I see your media kit" request with a personal response in addition to the PDF attachment.

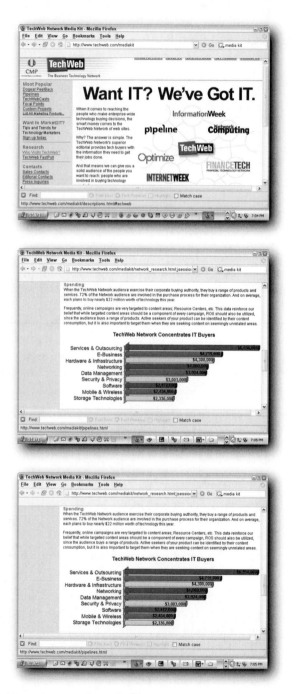

FIGURE 2-6: Sample media kit

Also, *before* you send out your media kit, do a little research on the potential buyer. It's always a good idea to find out who they represent and what their advertising goals are. This way, you can both qualify and tailor your response to them.

Finally, the people you can safely send your media kit to are media buyers, ad networks, dedicated sales forces, and anyone who looks like they have a genuine interest in and the ability to advertise on your site. It's often easy to get caught up in the excitement of outside interest, but remember that most inquiries yield no sales, and those are the ones who are qualified and not just some lookee-loo kicking tires.

Print Advertising Versus Web Advertising

I'm sure some readers are wondering what bearing print advertising has on a book that explains how to make money via the Web. It's important that we examine print advertising because most of the practices and metrics found in the business of Web advertising come from the print world. Print channel advertising (newspapers, gazettes, magazines) has been evolving since the 1700s, and a lot of lessons were learned along the way, lessons that apply to the Web.

The practice that was ported over from print advertising (and broadcast advertising to some extent) to the Web with the least modification is that of gathering demographic data, which we just covered. Another important practice is that of placement analysis; that is, valuating specific locations on a given Web page for their effectiveness in delivering a message to the reader.

There are four prime locations in a magazine for print advertising: the back cover, the inside front page, the inside back page, and the double-page spread dead center of the publication. Magazine publishers have learned that these spots seem to have the highest impact on reader attention. They also learned that full-page ads in other locations are more effective the closer they are to the front of the magazine, and right-hand full page ads are more effective than ones on the left-hand side. This is why media buyers will send in a FP4C (full-page four-color) ad with the instructions "RFFF" or "Right-Facing, Far Forward."

Similar studies have been done on Web pages, and although the most effective zones on a page can drift here and there depending on the layout, in general the most oft-read (or "hottest") zone is the top band of any page, with the top-left corner taking first place. Advertisers know this, and thus are willing to pay more money for their ads to run in an "above the fold" location, which means anything that the reader can see without scrolling down (the higher the better).

Creating Web (Banner) Ads

The process of creating banner advertisements (or just "banners") is markedly less involved than creating one for a print publication. Assuming you have the ad copy and artwork completed — arguably the most difficult part of creating any kind of advertising — creating a banner ad involves a bit of time in front of a graphics application such as Adobe ImageReady or PaintShop Pro, and you're done. Print ads require the creation of film (four negatives — called "separations" — for a full-color ad, one each for the CMYK colors — Cyan, Magenta, Yellow, and blacK), then color-proofing with a match print. Although you won't have any control over what colors your readers will see in your ads because monitors display colors with huge variance, you won't have to lay out the not-insignificant dollars for the separations. Also, if you need to change the wording or art in a banner ad, you'll find the cost of pixels to be infinitely less expensive than the cost of reproducing the separations for an ad.

But banner ads aren't all glory and sunshine. They do have disadvantages, including some particularly serious ones. Perhaps their greatest weakness is their relatively low effectiveness. After a few years on the Web, surfers become "banner blind." They stop seeing the ads entirely, even if they know that they're there. It was this drop-in banner ad effectiveness that triggered the creation of epilepsy-inducing ads such as the infamous animated "Punch the Monkey" banner and the ads created in neon colors that pulsed with a strobe-like effect. The advertisers in their less-than-Machiavellian wisdom figured that if the problem was a lack of reader attention, the solution was running banners constructed from hot pink and blazing neon green in their faces. Although these ads did see a decent spike in responses initially, they were also among the most reviled of banner ads on the Web, and people eventually began avoiding sites that ran them.

Another disadvantage banner ads have that print ads don't is that they can be blocked. When you read a magazine, unless someone has torn out the ads beforehand, you'll see them. You might not read them, and they may not influence you, but you will see them. Ads on the Web can be blocked by the more industrious, although maintaining the files necessary to block ads from every Web site that they eventually visit is moderately tedious. This is perhaps the most important reason as to why ad-blocking isn't more prevalent — most people just couldn't be bothered. For those of us who rely on banner ads to generate revenue, this is not something to be taken for granted.

Web Advertising Formats

Anyone who has spent more than a few hours on the Web will have noticed that there seem to be dozens of different ad sizes. The truth is that there are currently a bit over a dozen different "ad units" or sizes of ads that are commonly used. You can see all of the latest changes and standards (in the sense that advertisers have agreed on commonly accepted choices) at the Interactive Advertising Bureau Web site at `http://www.iab.com/` (see Figure 2-7).

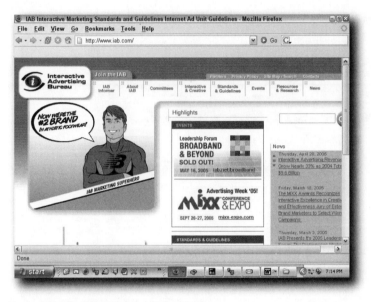

FIGURE 2-7: The Internet Advertising Bureau

The IAB is a standards body that seems to reflect common practices rather than develop and dictate standards. It also, according to its self-proclaimed mandate, acts as an advocacy body to protect and strengthen revenues for online concerns that use advertising as a way of generating money. Regardless of its intentions or philosophies, the IAB is certainly a useful reference site for people who run media channels. I recommend visiting the site on a weekly basis.

Static Web Advertising

Static ads are the most common type of banners to be found on the Web. They are of varying unit sizes, and may be animated, but don't use Flash, audio, Quicktime, or any other "rich media" features. Animations are limited to what a GIF file can do.

The very first static ads were just called *banners* and were 468 pixels long by 60 pixels high (from hereon, an ad's dimension will always be in pixels, and will always use the *length x height* format). They were sold for exorbitant sums and were worth every penny, because the Web was so new and ads were even newer, that Web surfers read and clicked on everything that was put in front of them. Today, the 468×60 banner is so ineffective that a lot of sites don't even bother serving them. (See Figure 2-8.)

FIGURE 2-8: The long-in-the-tooth 468×60 banner ad

The heir-apparent to the banner is the *leaderboard*, another long, rectangular ad that boasts a much larger area at 728×90. When placed at the top of a Web page (which is their traditional zone), this ad unit sees considerably greater success than the old banner. It is, as of this writing, one of the most popular ad sizes because it is not overwhelming, yet has enough area to communicate a more complex message effectively (see Figure 2-9).

Another very popular ad unit is the *large rectangle*. It is also called the *cnet box*, because cnet.com helped make the format popular by offering them on its enormous network of sites (see Figure 2-10). At 336×280, the unit provides plenty of area for creative ad design and yet remains reasonably sized. However, it and its smaller brethren are oddly enough shaped that if you intend to offer them, I recommend that you build your site around them rather than the converse. It's easy to place a leaderboard at the top of any site; it's difficult to introduce a cnet box or other tall rectangles to a page unless you already have a column that is or is very close to their pixel width.

FIGURE 2-9: The popular "Big Man on Campus" leaderboard

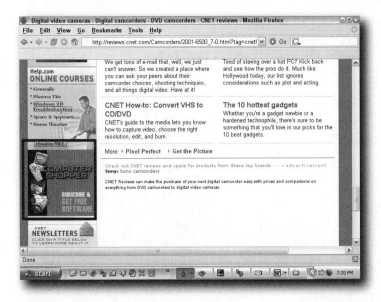

FIGURE 2-10: The effective, oddly shaped rectangle—always invited to parties, but never has any friends

Skyscrapers are tall, skinny ad units usually found in the left-hand or right-hand columns of Web pages (see Figure 2-11). They can be found in two sizes: the *traditional skyscraper* at 120×600, and the *wide skyscraper* at 160×600. There is also a new unit known as the *half page ad* that is 300×600. The original skyscraper is a fairly inoffensive-sized ad; it tends to not be particularly effective because it is most commonly located right beneath a Web page's navigation menu on the left-hand side, which means it is most often located "below the fold" (you have to scroll down to see it). The wide skyscraper suffers from the same problem, but both ad sizes remain moderately popular because they take up space that would normally remain empty. Some sites, particularly ones with a lot of content found on a single page (such as a news site), find skyscrapers entirely useful because their readers do tend to scroll down and thus eventually see the ads.

FIGURE 2-11: The tall, skinny skyscraper—the online advertising wallflower

The half-page ad at 300×600 is shockingly large. It is no doubt highly effective because it would be difficult to ignore, but it's difficult to fit into a page layout and it's so large that a lot of readers would be immediately turned off by the ad. I *do not recommend* offering this ad unit on your site unless you have data that shows your readers are willing to tolerate it.

In 2003, the IAB categorized two rectangles, one banner, and one skyscraper size as components of the *Universal Ad Package*. This is an attempt to reduce the number of ad units in use on the Web so that the costs associated with inefficiencies can be reduced. Whether or not the IAB has been successful in this is difficult to say at this point.

The ad units being promoted as part of the "standard package" by the IAB are the Medium Rectangle (300×250), the Rectangle (180×150), the Leaderboard (728×90), and the Wide Skyscraper (160×600). If you're planning your site's layout, keep these ad units in mind. If your space is limited and you're not sure which skyscraper to include, choose the larger of the two. It's much easier to sell ad space that allows for larger units than the smaller ones, with the exception of the very new and very controversial half-page unit.

Static banners are largely tolerated on the Web because they aren't overly offensive. They don't try to take over the browser and, in fact, behave like other graphics on any given Web page. Although they aren't the most effective form of Web advertising, they do seem to trade off by being generally accepted by the Net at large.

Rich Media Web Advertising

"Rich Media" is the buzzphrase used by the advertising industry to describe online ads that include audio, video, flash animations, or pretty much anything that goes outside the bounds of a static ad. These ads are more than just simple visual executions of an advertising message; they're noisy or flashy executions of advertising messages. Occasionally, the ad will be interactive; it will require running your mouse pointer over it to trigger the audio, for example (see Figure 2-12).

Advertisers generally love Rich Media ads. They do attract more attention and cause more *clickthrus*. Rich Media ads really stand out on a page, and, in some cases, are magnificent examples of eye-candy.

But readers don't like them much. Rich Media ads can be startling, especially when audio is involved. Readers don't like it when a Rich Media ad begins making, say, lightsaber noises, particularly when they're at work. Of course, you shouldn't be cruising the gaming sites at work anyway, but you get the point. Audio-enabled Rich Media ads sometimes attract unwanted attention.

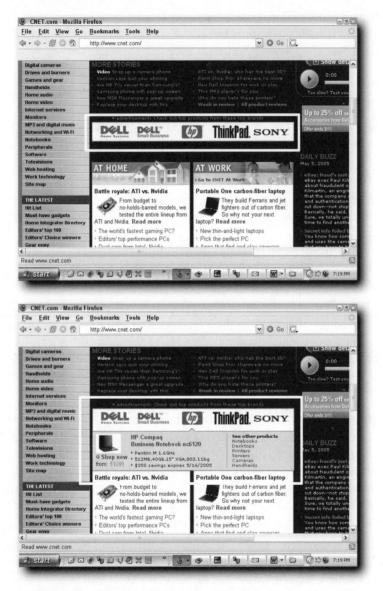

FIGURE 2-12: Note how the ad expands in "B" when you run your mouse pointer over it

You'll find Rich Media ads in all of the largest ad unit sizes (336×280, 728×90, 160×600) as well as a few of the medium-sized ones. I don't recommend against running any Rich Media ads, but I suggest that you do so sparingly. Unless you're running a site that attracts an audience who loves having their browser make all kinds of noises and appear to be under the thrall of a neon-dressed sorcerer, you'll find most readers are less likely to return if they constantly face Rich Media on every single page of your site without fail.

Of course, on the plus side, Rich Media ads will usually net you more money than static ones. Balance this one carefully and pay attention to the feedback from your audience.

As of this writing, there is some evidence that the majority of ad units being sold on the Web are in fact Rich Media, and as a result the term may be starting to phase out entirely. This has to do with broadband penetration in the U.S. surpassing the halfway mark — agencies see this as a *carte blanche* to up file sizes and creative content within an ad unit. Speaking as both a site owner and someone who has worked in creative direction, I'm more inclined to be careful about how quickly that envelope is pushed.

Pop-Anything Advertising

Without a doubt, *pop advertising* (which encompasses pop-ups, pop-unders, eye-blasters, and really anything that takes over the browser) is the most loathed form of advertising on the Web. Readers hate them with a passion that can rival the fire of a thousand suns. And yet, they are without fail the most effective form of advertising on the Web.

This strange dichotomy is common in online advertising. The more intrusive the ad, the more likely it'll be noticed and, therefore, the more effective it is. People click on the intrusive ads more than they do on the non-intrusive ones. However, the more intrusive the ad, the more flack you'll get as a site owner. And if you run pop-ups or eyeblasters, you'll need to really be careful about it lest you utterly demolish your audience numbers.

Pop-ups were the very first spawn of the evil that is pop-advertising. The surfer visits a Web site and some very insidious JavaScript causes a new browser window to open with the ad within it. The browser window can be positioned anywhere on the screen, at the whim of the coder. Some sites descend to a level of rudeness that is unmatched in the annals of history: They pop up several new ads when you close any one of the original windows. Try to close a second-generation window and several third-generation windows pop up. You can see where this is going. It's irritating and, ultimately, embarrassing for people who visit porn sites at work.

As I mentioned before, pop-ads are highly effective, and as such you'll be offered quite a bit more money to run these than if you were to only run static ads. Balance your desire for profit very carefully against the potential destruction you'll do to your audience if you go this route. A lot of advertisers have become wise to the effect pop-ads have on readers, so they'll often put a "cap" on them, limiting only one pop-under or pop-up per unique IP address per day. And yet, sometimes even this isn't enough. Readers really do despise this form of advertising. This is why there's such a big market for pop-up blocking software (which is now offered for free as part of Firefox and Internet Explorer).

Pop-ups are the oldest, least-effective of the "Evil Three" in this category of ads. They appear over or to the side of the reader's main browser window. Pop-unders are considerably more effective and sneaky to boot. They appear underneath the main browser window so surfers usually don't notice them until they close or minimize their browser. By that time, they've probably visited several sites, and it's difficult to figure out which one triggered the pop-under.

Finally, the most heinous of the three are known as "eyeblasters" or "floaters" (an allusion to toilet humor here that is hysterically accurate when you ask surfers their opinions of them). These are ads that travel and/or appear on top of the content in a browser window, usually keeping the content obscured for a fixed time, say 30 seconds, before they vanish on their own (see Figure 2-13). Scrolling does no good, because the ad maintains its absolute position within the frame of the browser window. Although the money offered for a "floater campaign" (see, I can't stop laughing) is usually quite excellent, you can bet that you'll instantly drive away a large percentage of your audience. It's just too easy to click away from a page that annoys you.

FIGURE 2-13: The floating ad—born in a wretched hive of scum and villainy

If by now I haven't convinced you that running this category of advertising is rife with consequences and horrid nightmares, do at least remember that keeping your readership mostly happy will probably net you more money in the long run.

Interstitial Advertising

An *interstitial ad* is one that interrupts the normal flow of navigation on a Web site with a full-page advertising message (see Figure 2-14). For example, you could be on the home page of a newspaper. You see the first paragraph of an article that interests you, and you click the `<continue to rest of article>` link. Instead of taking you to the page with the rest of the article, you see another page load, one with an advertisement on it. In some cases, there'll be a link that says `click here to continue` and in other cases you'll have to wait for a preset time before the site forwards you to the correct page. The ad may be a simple static banner, but these days it's likely to be Rich Media of some sort.

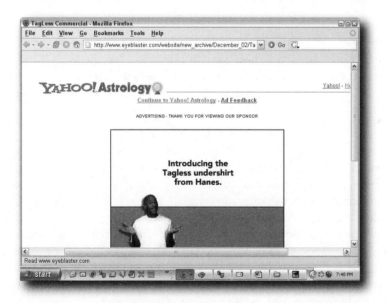

FIGURE 2-14: The interstitial or "commercial break" — and now for these messages. . .

`Salon.com` uses this ad format to great effect. You have two choices if you want to read any of its premium content: either pay for a yearly subscription or earn a 1-day pass. To earn the pass, you have to click on a link and sit through a 30- or 60-second Rich Media interstitial ad. Once you've done this, you receive a cookie that allows you access to Salon's subscription-only content for 24 hours.

Advertisers love interstitials. They love them because they're quite effective and their ad dominates the reader's screen because it's the only one there. They'll even pay pretty good money for them; generally better than plain banners, but not as much as pop-ads.

Readers, on the other hand, have mixed feelings about interstitials. It seems to be split about 50-50, anecdotally speaking. You'll have to run a survey asking about their tolerance for interstitials to get a realistic gauge of your own audience, but generally you can expect roughly the same numbers supporting and decrying your use of the ads. This ad type is tolerated more than pop-ads because they don't sneak on to your machine, nor do they actually obscure content—they briefly interrupt it. Something in the human psyche forgives this more easily than a blob that sits on top of the cartoon or text you want to read.

My recommendation for interstitials is to use them in one of two ways: either use them very sparingly in conjunction with other ad types, or use them moderately (say, serve one interstitial every 20 pages loaded per reader) all by themselves.

Text Ads

There's no doubt text ads are the most easily tolerated ads on the Web. Readers love them because they're easy to ignore and they take less time by several orders of magnitude to load. Don't forget that there are still millions of Internet users who use dial-up.

Advertisers generally aren't thrilled with text ads, unless they're served contextually, a la Google and Yahoo. Google hit on a really powerful and compelling business proposition by offering text ads within the context of a search or the dominant content on a page. It only figures that someone searching for "Mexico sightseeing" just might be interested in travel offers to Mexico. When you get your search results, Google (or Yahoo) also serves up text ads for any advertiser who paid for spots when "Mexico" and "sightseeing" are keywords in a search. This is called *targeted advertising*, and is found to be very effective. Anyone looking for something via a search engine is revealing their interests at that given moment to the search company—it only makes sense that an ad offering them a bargain on their current interest would be of more appeal to them than some random ad.

Google (and now other companies) have stretched their wings with text ads and now provide site owners the ability to run contextual text ads. Google's AdSense (`https://www.google.com/adsense/`) is an ad network that provides site owners with a stream of text ads keyed to content on any given page of a site. It costs nothing to join, and if you have significant traffic, it's possible to earn hundreds of dollars a month. There is a downside, which is part-and-parcel of the Cost Per Click (CPC) business model. More on that later in this chapter.

Even though text ads aren't intrusive, they seem to have a higher effectiveness largely because a lot of readers have not learned to automatically block them out of their peripheral vision yet. There is some argument to be made that text ads are, if nothing else, at least the most polite form of advertising from the vantage of the reader. Text ads are also much more limited in space, so the "copy" (advertising lingo for promotional prose) has to be very tight and focused.

If you're going to run contextual ad campaigns via Google or Overture, you need do nothing more than what you would normally do to run standard banner ads. Once you receive all of the information and tags that you require from the network, you implement as usual and let the campaigns run. AdSense (or whichever network you go with) does all of the hard work of figuring out which ads to send your readers by on-the-fly checking of the content on the pages in question (see Figure 2-15). If the content on your page has to do with *Star Trek*, you can bet there'll be text ads for *Star Trek* memorabilia, *Star Trek* DVDs, and posters of whoever the hottest *Star Trek* actress is at that moment. If you're running a forum and the latest discussion is on ending a relationship, I'd wager you'll start seeing ads for sites that market Russian brides.

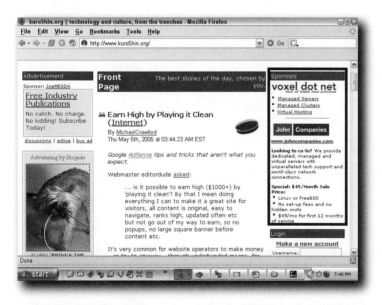

FIGURE 2-15: Now that's polite — not extremely effective unless you're using a search engine, but polite.

Keep in mind that occasionally you won't see entirely appropriate text ads for a given page. Ad networks can only serve ads for what they've been paid for. If you run a site that focuses on the mating habits of green-crested Northern Chickadees, it's likely you'll at best get ads for birdwatching books or perhaps the World Wildlife Fund. Sometimes there'll be no match whatsoever, and in those cases a network like AdSense will run Public Service Announcements (PSAs), or free ads for charities that net neither you nor the network any money.

My recommendation for text ads: Use them freely, but keep an eye on how well you're doing for revenue. Turn them down a bit if you're not getting much return on them. These are great fillers for ad inventory that hasn't been sold for a CPM deal or if you're just starting out and have no other ads to fill up your pages.

E-mail Advertising

If you have content that you can e-mail to people on a regular basis (for example, a daily cartoon strip, a monthly newsletter, or a weekly column), you have an opportunity to derive revenue from selling ad spots in the e-mails you send out (see Figure 2-16).

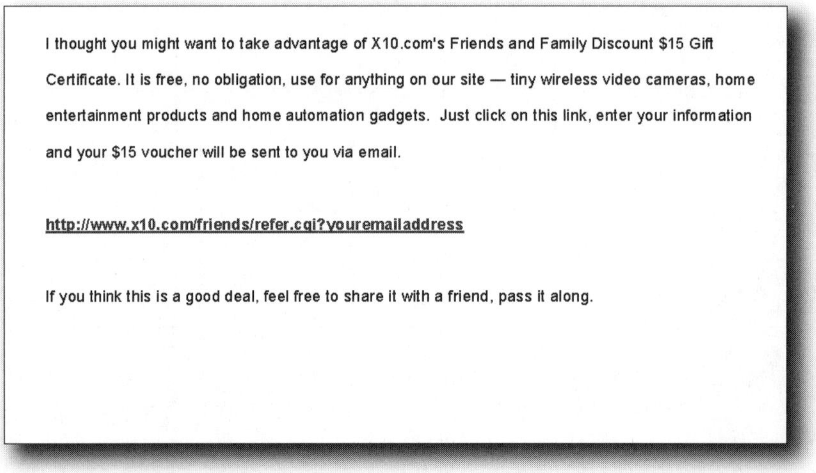

I thought you might want to take advantage of X10.com's Friends and Family Discount $15 Gift Certificate. It is free, no obligation, use for anything on our site — tiny wireless video cameras, home entertainment products and home automation gadgets. Just click on this link, enter your information and your $15 voucher will be sent to you via email.

http://www.x10.com/friends/refer.cgi?youremailaddress

If you think this is a good deal, feel free to share it with a friend, pass it along.

FIGURE 2-16: Sample e-mail ad

This is *not* spam. Spam is a loathsome practice and an enormous waste of other people's money and resources. The 2005 sentencing of a spammer to nine years in a Federal prison was met with some pleasure. Although I think that prison time was a bit much — a huge fine and years of probation would've been more appropriate — it does reveal exactly how frustrated we as a society are with spam in general. Electronic junk mail is hated more than regular, physical junk mail because the former costs the spammer little to send, and pushes the burden of cost and reduced productivity on the receiver.

The difference between spam and legitimate e-mail advertising is that of a voluntary, explicit request on the part of the reader, also known as *opt-in*. Be careful when you see that term, however. Some less-than-ethical marketers consider readers who don't explicitly say "don't send me that" as opting-in; this is actually known as *negative option marketing*, a synonym for "we're going to turn your mailbox into a sewer so long as we can make money from it" — another loathsome activity.

But when readers check a box that says "yes please, send me your monthly newsletter," they are overtly asking you to e-mail your content to them. If you really want to stay aboveboard, it would be wise to add a mention of the fact that the content may be accompanied by a few ads. It never hurts to be honest, unless you're trying to make money in the short-term and don't care much about your credibility or future.

Ads that you can send along with your content won't generate a lot of dollars unless you also know who you are sending them to. An advertiser selling programming software will pay a lot more if it knows that of the 2,000 subscribers you have, 88 percent of them are coders by occupation rather than just some faceless audience. Assuming you've already had a survey done, you can apply the numbers for your entire audience to your subscription base with an acceptable degree of accuracy. If 50 percent of your audience is female, it's not a reach to say that 500 (or thereabouts) of the 1,000 e-mail subscribers you have are also female.

Some site owners make the vast majority of their revenue with e-mail advertising. Over time they've built up a subscription base in the many thousands, and take regular demographic surveys to keep track of who is reading their content. Advertisers love this kind of advertising vehicle, because the readers have made it clear that they want the content and they'll open the e-mail when they get it.

I recommend this form of advertising very highly, but you do need to build up a decent subscription base (at least 1,000 subscribers, and even that's pushing it) and collect demographic information.

Podcast (Audio) Ads

Podcasting has become quite a rage in the past year, thanks to the proliferation of Apple's iPod. This form of media is akin to taping your favorite radio show and playing it back later, except in podcasting the show isn't usually aired live. You simply download and play the show at your convenience.

The most obvious form of advertising to be used in the podcasting medium is the audio commercial, just like you hear them on the radio. Many media buyers, always ready to examine new ways and means to conduct the campaigns in their charge, are prepared to buy into this channel. The most common advertising units thus far appear to be 15- and 30-second audio commercials, placed in break periods between the content. Because of the "newness" of the format (it isn't *really* new because radio has been doing this forever, but the novelty of podcasts does have an impact), there is little in the way of industry-standard pricing and practices. However, buyers have been paying based on the number of download requests for a given podcast per unique IP. And again, the media buyers are interested in knowing *who* these downloaders are. A media buyer for an IBM campaign will pay quite a bit more for 10,000 downloads made by a technocentric audience rather than a general one. If your show is largely technical, you can bet most of your listeners are, too, but are they all students or Chief Technical Officers? Get your demographics data collected!

Serving Ads for Fun and Profit

First of all, let's get something out of the way. There is nothing inherently evil about commerce. Trade is what makes this world go around. We all need to eat and have a roof over our heads. We are entitled to make money where and as we can. This entitlement does stop when you begin harming another (which is what criminal law is designed to punish), but as long as you are honest in your intentions and dealings, you are doing nothing wrong or immoral.

I bring this up because there is a very odd and very mistaken mentality that was prevalent on the Web in the late 1990s. This mentality believed that any monetization of content (particularly entertainment) was sleazy, evil, and immoral. Running ads on a site that you support with your own cash and sweat was considered dishonorable. If you dared ask for money to help out, you risked a metaphorical lynching!

This thinking comes from a corrupted version of the original goals of the early Internet, long before the advent of the Web. USENET kicked off in 1979, and from it arose a spirit of information sharing and discussion. The saying "information wants to be free" was adopted by USENET users; their intent was that information useful in research and the advancement of knowledge, science, and culture should be readily available to all.

A later generation adopted this saying as well, but twisted it to mean all content on the Web should remain free of advertising and free of charge. It's obvious where this thinking comes from. It's clearly self-serving, and it supports the selfish "gimme" attitude found in a good number of Net users.

It is with some relief that I've noticed a significant shift in that kind of thinking over the past few years. Right now, it's perfectly acceptable to the vast majority of readers if you run (non-intrusive) ads on your site, and acceptance also reigns for site owners who offer paid memberships. This shift really gained momentum shortly after the dot com bubble began to burst in 2000. A lot of readers began to realize that There Ain't No Such Thing As A Free Lunch.

There still remains a small percentage of Net users who abhor advertising (to the point of running and maintaining ad blockers) and who refuse to pay a single red cent (actual or in kind) for any content they consume. Thankfully for content providers everywhere, these people are to be found largely on the far ends of the bell curve.

Ad Serving: Yours or Theirs?

This is a question you'll have to answer based on what your needs and wants are. Should you run your own ad server or use one from a third party?

If you run your own ad server, it's assumed you know how to get Web software up and going. It's also assumed that you know how to fix problems (or can find someone who can help you fix them) if your ad server coughs up a hairball. You will have to learn how to use the software and how to optimize campaigns with it. In other words, it's a not-inconsiderable investment in time and money.

Using a third-party server has all kinds of bonuses. All you need to learn how to do is add their ad-serving "tags" (a block of code) to your Web site in the locations you've determined will be devoted to advertising. The third party (such as Google with its AdSense network) foots the bill for the software, maintenance, hardware, and does all or most of the optimizing. The only thing you need to concern yourself with is whether or not you need to bring in other ad networks.

Third-party servers, however, also take away most of your control when it comes to advertising. You can't decide to run ads you may have for another site you own unless the third party has a provision for it. You're at the mercy of whatever the ad network decides to send you. You can't, on a whim, decide to change the ads that are distributed during a given day or week. Ultimately, you're just renting out space to someone, and the rent amount is more often than not quite random.

Running your own ad server lets you take control of all of these factors. You can still run third-party ads (such as Google's AdSense) by placing their tags in the appropriate fields in your ad server software. You can also run your own campaigns to help sell your own memberships, merchandise, and events, and the number of ads you run for yourself is entirely up to you.

Another beautiful thing running your own ad server gives you is the ability to collect and analyze your own reports. When a campaign is run, you'll almost always be paid on the ad network's numbers (that is, they keep track through their third-party tags on your site as to how many impressions and clickthrus they get), but you'll have your own numbers to compare. If there's a huge discrepancy, it's time to do a little investigating in an effort to find out whether the ad network's server isn't tracking a campaign correctly.

There's a quirk about ad servers that you should be aware of. Serving ads can be a complicated business given the variations of daily ad impressions and problems with actually delivering all of the ads sent out. You rarely ever get all of the ads you mean to send out in a given day actually sent. Ad servers, therefore, try their best to serve ads as close to the requirements as possible, recalculating the rate of serving every hour or even more frequently in an attempt to hit the exact number of ads to be served. Invariably, you'll find that your ad server will deliver a bit over what is required, which is far more preferable than underdelivering. Advertisers don't care much if you serve a few too many of their ads, but they get cranky when you don't serve what you promised. It makes them less likely to want to do business with you again in the future.

I recommend that you stick to third-party servers until you start getting significant audience numbers — say, a million pages plus per month — or until you see some steady and significant revenue coming your way from your site. I use AdvertPro (`http://www.advertpro.com/`) at UF and only have good things to say about it. If you're not much into setting up a separate server and maintaining yet another piece of software, you can always opt for its AdvertServe offer (`http://www.advertserve.com/`), which gives you all of the power of your own ad server but is run as a virtual instance and is maintained by the AdvertPro people.

Ad Serving Jargon: What the Heck Did They Just Ask Me?

Like just about any kind of specialized field, ad serving has its own jargon. Say that an ad network contacted you and asked, "I need to serve a half million impressions over four weeks and can offer you a $0.60 CPM net, but I need a roadblock on Mondays between 0800 and 0900, can you deliver?" What would you say?

Ads on the Web are usually sold in chunks of 1,000, which means a thousand "impressions" or appearances of a given message. (Note that if you serve two ads on a page, that's two ad impressions you serve every time you serve one page impression.) The term *CPM* means "Cost Per Thousand," (the "M" coming from the Roman numeral for 1,000). The term comes from the print publishing world, where prices for an ad are dictated based on a publication's circulation numbers.

Now, just because ads are sold on a CPM basis doesn't mean that you can buy just a thousand impressions from anyone who has ads to sell. Most sites will have a "minimum buy" or amount that they're willing to run a campaign for; when you're running your own ad server, you'll understand why this is the case. It can be fiddly work, and handling buys of $10 at a go can be a frustrating and ultimately unprofitable way to go. As a rule, I don't accept buys worth less than $500. I recommend you set your own minimum buy and stick to it.

When an ad network offers you a campaign it'll give you the value of the buy as *gross* or *net*. Net is the more interesting number, because this is what you'll actually receive as the site owner. Most ad networks will skim about 50 percent off the top as their commission, so if they send you the gross value of a buy, you need to discount that by half (or whatever their commission is) to see what few coins will land in your lap. So, a $0.60 CPM net means that the ad network will pay you 60 cents per thousand ad impressions you serve, and they want to run a half million impressions. The campaign is, therefore, worth $300 to you.

The last part of the ad network's lingo-filled request involves something called a *roadblock* (also known as a *Take-Over*). This means that between 0800 and 0900 on every Monday during the campaign, the network wants only its ads to show up on your site, effectively "roadblocking" everyone else's ads. Today's ad-serving software has the ability to handle this function with a few clicks, so you don't need to worry about wrangling the software to take care of this. Also, other ad networks running their campaigns on your site won't object to a competitor's roadblock provided you still meet the target delivery numbers you promised them. On occasion, you'll get a request from a network or buyer asking for top priority, which means they want their ads to take precedence over any others; this bars roadblocks from other ad networks, and is usually worth an extra premium to you as the site owner.

Google's AdSense and most text ad campaigns on the Net run on the CPC revenue model. So do a lot of banner campaigns, from the plain vanilla static ones all the way to the other end where the bandwidth-heavy Rich Media interstitials reside.

CPC stands for "Cost Per Click" and is exactly what it sounds like. If a network offers you a buy of up to 20,000 clicks at a CPC of $0.15 net until December 15, they'll pay you 15 cents per "clickthru" on their ads, and up to a ceiling of 20,000 clicks or December 15th, whichever comes first. When either requirement is reached, number of clicks or the end date, the campaign ends.

Fifteen cents per click for up to 20,000 clicks equals $3,000 to you, an attractive sum indeed. However, keep in mind that if only a few people click on the ads, you could end up only getting a few dollars for your trouble. Given that the average ad clickthru rate on the Net as a whole hovers between 0.1 percent and 0.01 percent, don't expect to make huge dollars on a CPC campaign.

The third common revenue model for ad serving on the Web is the *CPA* deal, or "Cost Per Action." This is much like a CPC campaign, except the site owner is not paid per click, but *per action taken by a reader*. An "action" is anything the advertiser defines it to be, although it usually means a registration, purchase, or commitment of some sort at the advertiser's site. This is the foundation of affiliate programs made popular by Amazon.com — you get paid only when the advertiser gets something tangible out of the transaction.

Be Prepared to Say No

For obvious reasons, advertisers love CPC and CPA deals, and dislike CPM deals. Whenever I consult for a company that is just moving into the realm of selling advertising impressions, I always recommend that they be prepared to politely decline all CPA and most CPC deals. This is usually met with surprise, a normal reaction from anyone who hasn't been bloodied in the advertising game.

Let's look at CPC and CPA deals a little closer. An advertiser promises to pay you 25 cents for every clickthru they get from a unique IP per day. Clearly, the more impressions of their ad that you serve, the more likely it is that you'll get a clickthru. So, during the defined period, you run a half million impressions of their ad. At the end of the campaign, you discover that their ad has generated a grand total of 100 validated (excluding clicks from the same IP in the same day) clicks. You've just earned $25!

That miserable number (and $25 is indeed a horrid amount for 500,000 banner impressions, translating to a CPM of 5 cents) isn't unusual for a CPC campaign. So what exactly happened?

- You were paid $25.
- You served half a million impressions for the advertiser.
- The advertiser received a half million impressions worth of brand exposure, even if people didn't click through.
- The advertiser had at least 100 people visit their site.

The part that isn't stated explicitly is that during the campaign, you, the site owner, *bore most of the risk*. You gave up a half million of your monthly impressions to the campaign. Clickthru rates are impacted by the product or service being offered, the creative quality of the ad, and the visibility of the ad because of placement. Two of those three factors are out of your control! If an advertiser uses poor creative in their ads, and you're paid on a CPC basis, you're the one that suffers for the advertiser's incompetence! The advertiser only pays you for the people that actually go to the advertiser's site. Any risk on the advertiser's part was minimal.

CPA campaigns are even worse — absolutely *all* of the risk is born by the site owner, because the advertiser doesn't pay a cent unless someone you send them pays for or signs up for something. Advertisers will gleefully offer up CPA campaigns; site owners should just as gleefully turn them down. You should almost always take CPM deals, because they're money in the bank no matter how poorly the campaign performs.

CPC deals aren't always bad. If you have some uncommitted ad inventory, plugging in a CPC campaign or three isn't a bad idea. CPCs at least force the advertiser to bear a little of the risk, and it's better to chance a few clicks here and there on otherwise extra inventory rather than not make any money at all.

During and just after the dot com crash, you couldn't find a CPM campaign worth more than 50 cents net. CPCs and CPAs were the rage, because the perception was the online advertising was in the tank. Since about 2003, rates have been climbing back up as lessons that were learned were put into practice. Nowadays, CPAs are usually worth $5 or more per action, CPCs are commonly around the $1 mark, and CPMs range from $0.50 to $25 (although most CPM deals at the upper range are cancelable by the advertiser for poor performance). CPMs for e-mail advertising can reach well over $100 for narrowly targeted audiences, and that's what you're paid *every time* you e-mail your subscribers the content and ads.

In print publishing, it's not easy to obtain a gauge of how well a specific print ad is doing to raise consumer awareness in any given publication. There are very few ways of measuring that, and most of those ways don't give the advertiser an accurate picture. Rather, advertisers would pay attention to rises in awareness and sales from an aggregate of their advertising efforts.

But on the Web you can measure some things down to the click. And just because you can, all of a sudden it's important that you do. It also gives advertisers a metric or six to measure cost versus response. The more spectral long-term benefits of advertising (such as brand awareness) are largely ignored on the Web because, just like in the print world, they can't be measured.

Now that so much more can be measured online, advertisers put their stock in the value of these metrics, even if those metrics may or may not have anything to do with the long-term effectiveness of their advertising. These metrics are considered the gold standard by advertisers and ad agencies, and until they change their minds about them, it is to that yardstick by which a publisher's site is measured.

Keeping the Client Happy

Let's say you're running an ad server. Let's say your site is in the process of serving a net $15 CPM campaign of 300,000 impressions over two weeks. Let's say that this is something you can accomplish, but it'll be a little tight.

You wake up in the morning all smiling and happy. You do your 15-second commute from your bed to your desk chair and launch your Web browser. Horrors! Broken ad images abound on your Web site! Your ad server appears to have shuffled off its mortal coil!

The first thing you need to do as a site owner is accept that this sort of thing will happen. There are no ifs about it — software is imperfect and things blow up. The second thing you need to do is learn how to make good on campaigns that explode. The good news is that most advertisers are amenable to this sort of thing, and that's because they know that blow-ups happen.

Doing a "make good" is a time-honored practice in the print publishing industry. If the wrong ad is printed in a magazine, the magazine will usually offer to print the correct ad in the next issue and give the advertiser a freebie ad in a following issue. The same can be done for online advertisers. Let them know that your ad server fell over, but you'd be pleased to offer them another run of banners, say an additional 20 percent of the original run. Most advertisers will be mollified by this, or they may ask you to give them extra impressions to run in an upcoming campaign, always a good thing because it simply means more business for you.

Show Me the Money

When the dust settles, you're going to all of this effort to make money. You've acquired the campaigns, delivered the ads, and made the advertiser happy. So, where's your payment?

In the business world (and advertising is no exception), all payments are made 30 days after the fact. Many ad networks will state terms of "Net 30" from the date of completion of a campaign. This means that you can expect a check to land in your mailbox within 30 days of your successful fulfillment of an ad campaign. Other ad networks insist on "Net 30 after collection," which means they pay you within 30 days of them receiving the money from the advertiser, and because the advertiser is probably operating on Net 30 terms with the ad network, you can expect to wait upward of two months before seeing a dime for that campaign you just completed. It should also be pointed out that if an ad network is slow on collections, you may not see your money for 90 days, 120 days, or even longer.

There isn't much you can do about this unless you're an 800-pound gorilla in the advertising world. A company like cnet.com can insist on better terms from media buyers simply because it controls access to such an enormous number of ad impressions to an important audience. For a little guy like me or you, going along with what is industry-standard is about the best we can hope for.

For the most part, however, you can at least rely on the money showing up. Most ad networks out there with any sort of history live and die on their reputation. If advertisers or publishers catch wind of any sort of skullduggery, the Net helps word spread fast. Doing a little background research on companies you're about to sign deals with should be *de rigeur*. The axiom of caveat applies to buyer as well as seller in the advertising world.

When the Ad Agency Becomes the Enemy

There is an odd phenomenon that occurs occasionally in the advertising world. I tacked this section on to the end because it's a bit of an addendum, but is worth your attention.

Most of the time, ad agencies will be your customer, whether directly or through an ad network or sales force. They will have specific requirements and will be very professional in their expectations and their obligations. For the most part, you'll welcome their attention.

If you're a content creator, however, there can come a time when your ability to create, coupled with your deeper understanding of your audience, will threaten someone at the ad agency. Remember that ad agencies, the full-service ones, handle everything for the client, from media buying to creation of the message and art. Sometimes they'll send you ad creative that you just know won't resonate with your readers. This means that the campaign will do poorly and you'll be facing a loss in revenue because they'll pull the campaign early. So, you contact their buyer and suggest a few changes in the creative in an attempt to fine-tune the message in a way that will result in a much higher success rate.

You can bet that if the buyer takes your recommendations back to creative team who came up with the original ad, you'll risk never hearing from them again. What's happened is that the creative team will not want to appear incompetent or trumped by some lowly site publisher, and they fear losing out on a promotion or even being terminated. In our industry, our creativity is wrapped fairly tightly around our egos, and art directors and copywriters at ad agencies are no exception to this.

You should also be very careful about doing an end-run around ad agencies. At one point, UF was in talks with Compaq (just before its merger with Hewlett-Packard) over a full-featured sponsorship and year-long campaign to help push Compaq's profile up above the hardware market quagmire. After several face-to-face meetings involving a lot of air miles, Compaq's Vice President of Marketing and her entire team were nodding and smiling. A contract worth a very large sum indeed (I still weep at the number) was drawn up and we were prepared to sign.

The kink in this process popped up when Compaq's ad agency was brought in to manage the deal. Even though UF did all of the preliminary work, the ad agency was still to receive its full commission off the half million — something that I was perfectly fine with. We made it clear to the ad agency that they were in the driver's seat and we'd be ready to start the campaign and promotion on their signal. All we needed was the signed contract faxed over to us.

Weeks passed, then months. The ad agency kept coming back to us with minor changes here and there to the contract. Finally, they stopped returning our calls altogether. We got fed up and called Compaq's VP of Marketing — only to discover that she had been replaced with someone new, and that the replacement had never heard of us, and could we please talk to Compaq's ad agency instead?

It was clear to me what happened. The ad agency was feeling very threatened by this upstart of a Web publisher horning in on "their business" and took steps to squeeze us out of the picture. They were probably aware that the old VP was on her way out, and made sure that her replacement directed all media offers to them and only them. It was easy to do, given that the replacement had no relationship with us, and it didn't matter that they would be getting paid the same money if they had brought us to Compaq instead of us going direct to the client. This was about control and power, and the agency was categorically uninterested in giving up any of that power, even in perception.

When you're facing a heavy like an ad agency, it's best to just be as open and honest as possible. Don't ever be afraid to say no to them, but always try to remain diplomatic. Media buyers come and go, and you may find yourself having to start relationships over when a buyer you've been dealing with for the last year leaves. Also, remember that agencies and ad networks aren't evil — some of the people that work within them might be less than ethical, but be sure to judge people like that individually. Everyone is in this business to make money, and if you communicate that you share their objective and you have something to offer, you'll find yourself included in an industry that can keep you hopping and excited every day of your career as a content publisher.

chapter

in this chapter

The Membership Game

I don't care to belong to any club that would accept me as a member.

— *Groucho Marx*

Bethany was clever, and she knew it.

It all became abundantly clear one day while Bethany was enjoying her afternoon stroll. She took daily walks along her neighborhood roads because of all of the interesting things to be found. One particular favorite of hers was the farmer's market, where she could browse and sample the many wares that the artists and hobby farmers had to offer.

That particular day she came across a new stall, one she hadn't noticed before. An unimposing and pleasant-looking fellow stood behind it. She saw that he was offering toffees. An older couple was just leaving, toffees in hand, probably so that they could enjoy them later.

She approached the stall and looked at the large bowl. Toffees overflowed onto the stall. She reached for one.

"I hope you enjoy it. They're handmade. I make them myself."

The toffee-maker was smiling shyly. Bethany unwrapped the candy and popped it into her mouth. Flavor exploded as she chewed. "Wow."

"Is it good, then?"

"Delishush," she mouthed around the thick, sweet candy. Bethany loved toffees, but the ones you could buy in the shops were all rather bland.

She looked around for prices while she chewed. The toffee-maker smiled and shook his head. "They're free. I want everyone to try my toffees." He gestured at a sign above his stall. "The people at Dentascrub pay me a bit of money to show their flag here. That way I can afford to keep making toffees to give away."

Bethany thought that was rather clever of the fellow, and walked home chewing on the piece of candy.

For a few weeks, Bethany made it a point to stop by the toffee-maker's stall to get a piece of candy. The toffee-maker always greeted her with a shy smile.

And then it struck Bethany that rather than taking the time to walk over to the stall, she would instead train her pet cockatoo to fetch one for her every day. It would certainly save her some time. So, she set about teaching the fine-feathered squawker to gather a toffee from the toffee-maker's stall in the mornings. It didn't take her long to accomplish this, and soon enough she had a fine hand-made toffee delivered to her by winged courier every afternoon. She was feeling quite clever.

After several weeks had passed, Bethany heard a knock at her door. She opened it and outside on her doorstep was the toffee-maker. "Hello," he greeted her.

"Hello. What can I do for you?"

"Oh," replied the bashful fellow, "I noticed that my toffees were being carted off by a rather large, abrasive bird, and so I followed him today. It appears he's yours, and he's been nicking a toffee every day to deliver to you."

"Yes," said Bethany. "I don't know about him 'nicking' them though. I thought you said they were free."

"They are," replied the toffee-maker. "I don't insist people pay anything for them. But I rather depend on people coming by the stall to pick them up, so they can see my sponsor's sign and keep them happy. If they aren't happy, I don't get paid."

Bethany shrugged. "I don't much like signs. And I don't use Dentascrub, nor will I ever. Given that, what difference does it make if I see the sign or not?"

"The difference," said the toffee-maker, "is that Dentascrub keeps track of how many people visit my booth. It doesn't matter if you don't buy their stuff, or even look at the sign. What matters is that I can tell Dentascrub that so many people come by to have my toffees every day."

"Well," replied Bethany, "it's inconvenient for me to walk to your shop every day. I just don't have the time to spend. Anyway, good day." She shut the door on the toffee-maker, irritated that he'd have the gall to question her about taking his free toffees.

Bethany's cockatoo continued to fetch her toffees, and after another week had passed, she heard another knock on her door. It was the toffee-maker again.

"I don't mean to bother you, but I have a solution to all of this." He was holding a small box of toffees.

"I'm listening," said Bethany, her boredom clearly showing.

"It's clear you don't think much of the sign I have, so I thought, wouldn't it be nice to give people the ability to have my toffees yet not having to bother with the sign! So, what I did was put together another stall where there are no signs, and I have toffees there. But to get at them, you need a key to open the box. And," the toffee-maker said happily, "for a few dollars every month, you can have one of the keys to that box!"

"I don't quite see the point," replied Bethany. "Why would I want to pay you money for free toffees?"

The toffee-maker looked stricken. "Well, they were never truly free, you know. They do cost money to make, and the stalls cost money to rent. So, they're actually subsidized by Dentascrub. But it wouldn't be right for anyone to just take a toffee without in some way helping me keep my stalls open."

"I see," replied Bethany. "I'll give it some thought."

And Bethany did just that for a few minutes. She decided that she liked having her toffees for free, and delivered to her by a large, feathered bird that thought it was a pterodactyl. So she did nothing, and remained feeling quite clever.

And nothing changed for some more weeks, until one fine afternoon her cockatoo delivered to her something strange. It was a toffee, but not the usual. It tasted all right, but it didn't last long. It also had an odd texture.

So, she decided to take a walk to visit the toffee-maker, and perhaps give him a bit of a talking to. Changing the recipe without any notice would not be tolerated, and she would make that very clear.

When she turned the corner, she stopped in mild shock. Everything looked different. The farmer's market was gone. In its place was a huge retail store belonging to one of the big chains. Where the toffee-maker had his stall was a massive billboard declaring the virtues of Dentascrub. Beneath it was a large wire basket filled with bulk candies of all types, to which was tacked a sign: PLEASE TAKE ONE! COURTESY OF DENTASCRUB.

Bethany felt clever indeed.

I've used that parable to warn others about the dangers of consuming without giving back. "Little people" like you and I don't have the financial robustness to survive that sort of attitude for long. Large corporations (such as the mythical "Dentascrub") can simply "adjust strategies" and rest on their bank accounts for three or four quarters while they ramp up other ways to make money.

As was explained in Chapter 2, people generally don't like advertising. But people do like good content ("good" being defined as whatever each person subjectively feels is something appealing), and they'll keep coming back to consume that content. So, if, on the Web, selling advertising is the family member no one ever talks about, who's the golden child of the family?

You would think that *paid memberships* would be hailed by readers who hate ads. You pay for your consumption of a service or product, and the creator is compensated for his or her time, effort, and talent. It makes perfect sense and is perfectly fair, and yet. . .

On the Net, people don't pay for anything that they don't have to. The same people who don't think twice about paying $20 for some cheap light-up trinket at a department store will feverishly resist plunking down 50 cents for music or art or other forms of entertainment on the Web. And it has less to do with the virtual nature of the product than you might think. It has to do with transience.

During the very end of the twentieth century when the dot com era was in boom times, several enterprising people attempted to put together online malls — conglomerations of online retail Web sites under one virtual roof. Unfortunately for them, the mall idea never did take off, again because of transience. The fact is, there was no reason for anyone to shop at a particular online mall. Consumers just wanted access to specific retailers, and the malls those retailers were in were irrelevant. The transience becomes clear when you realize that *the rest of the Web is only a single click away.*

(Technically, this isn't completely true, because many pages are buried more than one link deep. However, leaving any site often only takes a single click. You can't do that in a real-life mall.)

The same goes for content on the Web. If you're offering content and you charge for it, you're going to be slicing away a very large chunk of your potential audience. People can be cheap, and self-centered. They'll get cranky if you skip posting your column for one day, but if you ask them for a couple of bucks a month to help prop you up, they'll look at you like you were from Neptune.

This mentality comes from a consumer's perception of value. Assuming you give them their content every day for free, why should they pay for it? Will they really care whether they have the word "Member" tagged on to their name in your forum or comment system? Because a visit to a Web site can be so fleeting, if you charge for your content, some of your readers will simply click themselves to a site where similar content is free.

Ultimately, people will pay money when they feel they're getting something in return. That something might be just a fuzzy feeling for supporting an effort that they feel is worthwhile (like a charity for homeless animals), or it might manifest itself as a tangible good that has some perceived value beyond the intrinsic (such as a t-shirt with original art on it).

Back in the days of the bulletin board systems (BBSs) when the Net was mostly populated by geeks and academics, a lot of social computing still took place. People clustered on their local bulletin board systems, dialing up (with acoustic couplers, which are a bit like retarded modems) one at a time to someone's computer in a basement and posting messages and replies. After thirty minutes or so of that, they would log off and the next person would log in and do the same.

Some of these BBSs arranged to have two or more phone lines coming in at once, allowing users to access them more readily and actually see new discussions appear posted by others while logged in. This sort of arrangement cost real dollars; the tariff for six phone lines was more than most hobbyists would want to pay. The System Operators (SysOps) of these BBSs appealed to their members for help in paying these bills. In return, they were given access to parts of the BBS restricted to paying members. Often, these were file libraries and exclusive forums, areas where the "paying elite" could take better advantage of what the BBS as a virtual locale and a social circle had to offer.

This serves to teach us that people are willing to pay for something exclusive. It also teaches us that people generally want something for their money above and beyond any "free" content that they're already consuming. I'll be discussing how to maximize your reach with regard to this a bit further on in the chapter.

One company that's done remarkably well as an online business is Amazon. Jeff Bezos' vision of a massive online mall (a mall that is an integrated whole rather than a loose collection of unrelated online retailers) where you can buy any current book under the sun and a lot of older books is taking shape despite the gloomy predictions of his detractors. (I have to admit that Amazon did give me some satirical fodder for my cartoon a few years back. Although I didn't directly take a poke at Amazon's business model, I feel Bezos made me eat my words in a very oblique way, and I can't say I'm too chagrined by it. It's nice to see an Internet success story after all of the failures.)

Let's have a quick look at the Amazon Web site. The most prevalent component on Amazon is the encouragement to spend money. This encouragement isn't direct or coarse. Rather, you're showered with deals, discounts, and special bargains. "Free two-day shipping!" "50% Off!" "$500 Back!" — these are all reasons why you would want to shop at Amazon and nowhere else. Plus, Amazon makes it easy to navigate through all of the nifty things you can buy, and even easier for you to pay them money. Amazon accepts every major credit card, checks and money orders, plus gift certificates. If you've bought into the ideals of consumerism, Amazon is a dangerous place to go unless you're also financially golden.

These lessons are useful to us even if we're not in the business of selling tangible items like books and DVDs. Amazon has cleverly maximized its retail channel not just by offering the customer a million options, but by offering the customer 10 or 20 of those options at a time. Amazon has made it easy for you and me to spend money there.

Let's examine these lessons and see how they can be applied to the Web site of a poor starving content provider. The difference between Amazon and people like us is that we're trying to sell, as a principal "product," a membership. Selling intangibles is generally more difficult than selling physical objects, but the way you sell them is similar in many ways that matter.

What Are They Really Buying?

You'll need to answer this question first and foremost. When one of your visitors buys a paid membership, what is he or she really buying?

When someone pays for a membership at UserFriendly (UF), at minimum two things happen:

- The word "Member" is appended to the username in the user's diary (a UF version of a personal blog), so "Diary of Katticus" would read "Diary of Member Katticus."

- The member has the capability to turn off the ads on the site from the user's account settings.

In other words, what I've given them for their money is public recognition (having "Member" tagged on to their diary) and reprieve from site advertising. As an aside, they also get an intangible known as the "fuzzies" — a good feeling for helping out a creator whose work they enjoy.

It'll be up to you as far as what you wish to give your audience in exchange for their money. Ars Technica (`arstechnica.com`) gives paying members access to other parts of the site, and to a private forum. It also tacks on "subscriptor" to the member's posts in both forums. Fellow cartoonist Bill Holbrook over at `kevinandkell.com` has a "Sponsor a cartoon for a day" offer. For $5.00, the sponsor's name appears below a cartoon for the day, along with a short message if they wish. Both Ars Technica and Bill Holbrook are offering virtual, intangible goods in exchange for money. The key here is that they're offering something from which the non-paying audience is excluded. Thus, the paying member is buying *exclusivity*.

This is important. If you, like most content providers, are offering your content (or at least the main body of it) for free, you need to offer something else that people can give you money for. People like to feel special, so when they send you the $5 or $20 or $100, you need to give them something in return that helps them do that.

This isn't to say that you can't raise money just by asking for it. The fabulous gang over at This Week In Tech (Leo Laporte, Patrick Norton et. al. from the old TechTV show *The Screen Savers*) are podcasting, and as of this writing, they have yet to run ads on their Web site or audio commercials within the podcasts. They simply asked their quite significant fan base for a couple of bucks each to help offset their costs and succeeded in raising a few thousand dollars in a very short period of time. However, unless you have a sizable audience like they do, don't expect the same results for yourself.

Holding Out a Hat Marked "Donations"

I'm only going to touch on donations briefly. If you cruise for content on the Web you'll inevitably run across an Amazon or PayPal button with "DONATE" blazed across it in thick, dark letters. I don't like donations for content creators for a couple of reasons. The first is that Amazon and PayPal are getting a cut of money that was really meant entirely for you. There are no other easy ways to collect donations on the Web I can think of, so I'm really protesting out of principle here.

The second more important reason is that asking for donations looks decidedly unprofessional. Unlike people watching buskers in the flesh world, there is little immediate connection between a reader and the artist on the Web. Donations are also another way of saying, "I have nothing else to give you." There's no exclusivity being offered.

So, when it comes to creating revenue streams, I strongly recommend you put limits on how long you have a donation button up. It might be acceptable at the beginning when you're just starting out, but if you're providing content to an audience of thousands, it looks amateurish. If people are giving you money, *you should give them something in exchange for it*. This is the fundamental element of commerce, or trade, and you're in business.

There's also the mentality surrounding donation systems that I feel can hinder your thinking when it comes to business. Relying on the goodwill of others makes for very poor business strategy. You need to remove the crutch and become proactive in attracting your audience's money.

What Should You Give Them?

This is one of those questions that have as many answers as there are people you ask. Some people like to be told what they should offer, but I'm against that idea as a creator writing for creators. Do you really want to run another cookie-cutter Web site with the same offer as 300 other Web sites one or two clicks away? I have faith that pretty much anyone who buys this book has enough creative energy to come up with some terrific offers that are specifically suited to his or her site and audience.

Something you should always be aware of is that even though you've given your audience access to your content without directly charging for it, many of them will *not* feel as if they owe you anything in return. Thus, when you offer paid memberships, the first question that will go through their minds is "What's in it for me?"

You absolutely *must* address this. Not only will it help attract them to your offer; it'll help make things clear in your mind as to what it is you're giving back in return for their money. A transaction is about to take place between you and Jane Audience-Member; she's going to give you money, and you're going to give her. . . what?

By now you're probably cognizant of the two general categories of things to offer your paying members: intangibles and tangibles. The former are online badges like "Member," or access to private parts of your site. The latter are physical items, perhaps t-shirts branded with your site logo or original artwork. What you need to decide is which of the two to offer, or perhaps you'd like to offer both.

Intangibles

Intangibles are attractive to site owners because their costs are generally low to non-existent. You throw a switch on your site and you've fulfilled your end of the bargain. There's no packaging, shipping, or tracking lost parcels. Also, there's little or none of your money involved up front in the purchase of any tangibles.

However, intangibles have a downside. They're generally harder to sell and finding the correct price point can be arduous. How much is the label "Gold Level Sponsor" worth anyway? (The answer is "however much people will pay for it." This is the basis for what is known as "functional pricing.")

If you're going to offer intangibles, first find out what it is your audience would respond well to. If some of them tell you that they'd be happy to send you five dollars for a tag like "Member," make sure that you can offer them that or something similar. Maybe this serves as a foundation for an entire scale of membership tags: "Member" could cost $5, "Patron" might cost $10, and "VIP" could cost $25. Don't be afraid to experiment and run focus groups with your audience. I'll show you how to do that in Chapter 6.

While you're mapping out your plans to get rich with your intangibles, you'll also want to consider factors such as term length and renewals. Is that $5 for the "Member" tag for life or one calendar year? If the tag expires after a fixed period, do your paying members get a discount on a renewal? What happens if you run a promotion for virtual membership tags? That 20 percent discount you're offering might attract more paying members, but how are the ones who paid full price two weeks ago going to feel? Whatever you choose to do, think about it carefully instead of just flying blindly into what seems to be a good idea. Successful businesses get that way because of a lot of thinking and planning. Get feedback from your audience, and listen to them. They hold the key to this part of the equation.

Just to remain legal and protected, you'll need to have your members agree to a "Terms of Service" (TOS) contract that specifies what it is they're getting for their money and what their and your rights are in the transaction. When it comes to intangibles, I highly recommend you use a "blood and guts" TOS — this is a contract that effectively protects you with iron-clad language. Once the money is transferred and you fulfill your end of the transaction, the member cannot ask for his or her money back. If you run into a situation where it might be expedient for public relations or just your peace of mind to refund someone their money, you can still choose to do so, but you should always use a TOS that says you don't have to.

You can find TOS contracts all over the Web; I have one tailored specifically for content creators at the Money For Content Web site at `http://www.money` `forcontent.com/` — feel free to use it as is or modified for your own specific purposes.

There's another intangible that I have yet to cover that is quite different from "features" such as a member tag or the ability to shut off the ads on your site: access to exclusive content. If you have the ability to create content above and beyond what you provide to the Net for "free," you might want to consider doing so and giving only your paying members access to that content. This can be a very compelling feature if you have a devoted audience. Not only does it satisfy the element of exclusivity, but you're also explicitly giving them something they perceive as valuable in return for their cash.

Tangibles

Tangibles (those things you can pick up and hold in your hands) are a bit of a different story. These require physical handling, packaging, and shipping. If you don't think this is a big deal, ask yourself why there are businesses that do nothing but fulfill orders for other companies.

The process of fulfillment (the shipping of physical goods to a consumer) is time- and labor-intensive. It works best in an assembly-line fashion and is a multi-step process: orders are taken, money is collected, shipping labels are printed, goods are picked and packaged, labels are applied, and the packages are mailed or couriered. Even if your tangible is only a t-shirt, you still have to go through all of those steps — and those steps don't even include sourcing and production of said shirts!

There are places on the Web that do this sort of thing for you, although mostly as a branding effort (something we'll get into in Chapter 5) and not really as fulfillment houses. Let's assume you're not intimidated by the amount of work involved and want to start small with a tangible item like a plastic membership card. I like cards because they're small, relatively inexpensive, and they are easy to package and ship. What do you have to do?

First of all, you have to source a supplier. There are quite a few on the Web and they'll take artwork in the form of a digital file. Once you find one you're happy with (again, you can find some help in this on the `moneyforcontent.com` Web site) you'll have to send them the artwork so they can give you a quote. You ask for a run of 500 cards to be produced and you pay for them. You now have 500 blank membership cards waiting at the supplier.

You open up your paid membership offer to your audience and in 30 days you collect 80 sign-ups. They've paid you their $20 apiece and have supplied you with their names and mailing addresses. You send the 80 names to the card maker and the names are embossed onto the cards — and you pay for the embossing. They're shipped to you, you print out shipping labels, put the correct card into the correctly labeled envelope, and off you go to the post office. You pay for the mailing and 80 envelopes head out to the world.

Note that in this example you didn't start a run of names to be embossed on the cards until you had collected a reasonable number. Whenever you personalize tangible goods, there are minimum production runs that can affect how quickly you can ship them. Personalization is a very good thing, however — you won't get as much interest in a membership card that doesn't have the member's name on it.

There's another issue surrounding tangible goods that is often overlooked (much to the chagrin of budding entrepreneurs): returns and customer complaints. What happens if the shipping address supplied was incomplete or mistyped? The package will come back to you, and you'll have to spend the time tracking down the member to obtain the correct address, and then you'll have to pay for more postage. What if you send the wrong item to the wrong people? One member gets a small t-shirt and the other gets an XL, and it should be the other way around? You won't know there's a problem until at least one of them contacts you about it, and if the other person doesn't say anything (say the recipient of the small shirt gives it to his or her child) you'll have to come up with another t-shirt and send that off in exchange for the one they send back.

I'm not trying to scare you into never, ever offering tangible goods as part of a paid membership. I just want you to be aware that it is a fiddly, labor-intensive business all on its own, and you need to be aware of the potential pitfalls. In fact, tangible goods make some of the most compelling offers for paid memberships, so they're often — not always — worth the extra effort.

The Sponsorship Drive

Something I've been using at UF for a few years now with solid success is the notion of the *sponsorship drive*. This is the same concept as it is used on PBS (http://www.pbs.org/) and other publicly funded services that draw little or no financial support from taxpayers. It has distinct advantages over a simple membership offer such as only occurring periodically, thereby increasing the perception of exclusivity.

Sponsorships also use a tier system. Let's use PBS as an example. When it has its television programming drives, it offers viewers somewhere between three and five different levels (or tiers) of sponsorship. The idea is that viewers who can afford more can pay for the higher tiers. The money paid goes toward future programming for PBS and its cost of operations, things that its viewers are happy to support.

Each sponsorship tier is given a title and a tangible that is sent to the viewer. The tangible is more often than not an exclusive, although occasionally the truly exclusive items are reserved for the topmost tiers in a sponsorship drive.

During one drive put on by PBS (it ran the drive between back-to-back episodes of the Britcom *Red Dwarf*), it offered four tiers. The breakdown looked something like this:

- $50 level — *Red Dwarf* t-shirt
- $150 level — *Red Dwarf* novels (6 books)
- $250 level — *Red Dwarf* episodes (8 VHS tapes)
- $750 level — Autographed *Red Dwarf* jacket

All of the items in the first three levels were available to the public from other sources — you didn't need to send PBS any money to obtain them. Clearly, PBS was relying on people seeing the value of supporting its programming as the major motivator for a sponsorship. The top tier offered a high-quality jacket that was autographed by at least one of the stars of *Red Dwarf*. The jacket itself, while stylish, was probably only worth about $250. Having it autographed at least doubled its value, but it was also an exclusive item you couldn't obtain anywhere else.

This psychology can be put to use in our efforts to make money as creators. If you run a yearly, semi-annually, or quarterly sponsorship drive, you can focus your efforts to obtain members during those periods. Run internal house ads, post news items, or insert a "house commercial" inside one of your podcasts urging your audience to consider sponsoring your work.

Any sponsorship drive should, by its very nature, have a limited time to run. At UF, my audience is made up largely of daily readers, but I have a significant number that comes to the site once a week or even once a month. They catch up on the content all at once in one sitting and then go away for another period of time.

Based on that, I run my sponsorship drives for roughly four weeks each. I have a drive three times a year, around every April, August, and December. I've fine-tuned the frequency and run time over the years, and you'll have to do the same until you get a proper feel for your audience. However, it's a very good idea to keep your drives on the spare side. Run one and then wait at least six months, unless you have direct indications that another one would do very well.

By the way, for the sake of this chapter, I stuck with calling a sponsorship drive just that, in imitation of PBS. For the sake of clarity, however, when you run a drive on your site, I recommend calling it a *membership drive* instead. Assuming you intend to have advertisers, the title *sponsor* should be reserved for someone or some company that pays you money to feature their product or service on your site.

The Question of Price Point

A *price point* is the ideal price for a product, or the top price the consumer is willing to pay for something. It's the magic number you as a seller want to find for your memberships; often it's a number you would never have imagined.

I have a friend who is a very talented potter. She could make exquisite ceramics and was quite prolific, and she opened a ceramics shop in a small town near where I live. She had priced many of her works in the $25–$30 range, and the response from her customers was disappointing. A mutual friend who specializes in retail told her to bump the prices up to the $50–$75 range. Despite her protests she did so, and suddenly she couldn't keep the ceramics on the shelves.

The lesson here is that when it comes to something such as art (like my friend's ceramics), intangibles or anything that people have an emotional bond with, you can charge more than you might think because of perceived value. I've been told many times by my readers that they're more than happy to pay me $36 a year for a membership at UF because not only do they enjoy the cartoon and the huge community that has grown around it, but they've met new friends, found jobs, and even discovered their life partners through my site. How do you put a dollar figure on that? Three dollars a month doesn't seem that much to ask for what UF seems to have given them.

Of course, your site isn't UF; you'll have your own distinct audience and you'll be offering them something that is uniquely yours. You'll need to gauge how much to charge and fine-tune the numbers as time goes on. Eventually you'll hit that price point.

Accepting Payment (or Keeping Your Hands Open)

One of the greatest and most fatal failings of any small business on the Web has to do with accepting payment. In a nutshell: *you must make it as easy as possible for people to give you money.*

I can't count the number of times I've seen something on the Web that I wanted to buy, opened up a shopping cart, proceeded to the checkout and. . . lo and behold, they didn't accept the method of payment I wanted to use. That killed the sale right then and there, because of the nature of the Web. I just clicked and went elsewhere.

You'll note that Amazon does a great job of this. Most links on the site lead to an item, and on every page with an item, there's at least one clear link to add that item to your cart and one clear link to have you immediately buy the item. When you're at the checkout, you'll note that Amazon offers you a fistful of different ways to pay, including second-tier credit cards such as Discover and Diner's Club.

The first time I ran a membership drive on UF there were only two ways to pay: PayPal or with a check or money order. When I added credit cards about a year later, the amount of money I raised in a single membership drive *tripled*. This significant increase makes plenty of sense when you consider that most adults have at least a Visa or MasterCard.

Let's have a look at the most common payment methods available on the Web and consider their advantages and disadvantages.

Checks and Money Orders

This is the oldest form of payment, and it still works for us Web people. You'll need to provide a mailing address, of course, and a form online that they can fill out, print, and send you with their check. I recommend obtaining a post office box unless you have no issue with making your real address public.

Keep in mind that checks, unless certified, can bounce. You'll want to hold off on sending your customers their goods until the check clears your bank. This can take up to ten business days, so be sure to figure that in to any shipping promises.

PayPal

PayPal (http://www.paypal.com/) has been in business since 1998 and was acquired by eBay Inc. (http://www.ebay.com/) in 2002. Although it claims to not be a bank (to avoid being regulated as a financial institution), it effectively operates as one, handling other people's money and taking a small percentage for all services as its fee. There is some controversy over PayPal's operations, and there have been some truly nightmarish stories coming out of PayPal experiences, where people's bank accounts have been frozen in their entirety during an investigation. You can get the full story from the gripe site NoPayPal at `http://www.paypalsucks.com/`.

Nonetheless, PayPal has become a bit of a standard on the Web for accepting payments. I've been using PayPal at UF for four years as of this writing and haven't had anything really bad happen to my account (knock on wood!). PayPal has done some annoying things, such as change the format of its purchase notifications eight times since I started using it. Not once did I or my system administrator receive any notice about the changes beforehand, and this caused UF's transaction server to barf. Ultimately, it meant having to go in and upgrade accounts by hand until the new code was in place on our end.

Don't forget that PayPal skims a fee, usually a flat amount plus a percentage, for each transaction. It's imperative that you figure this fee into your cost and profit calculations; you can give yourself quite a shock when you think you should have $500 in your PayPal account and you discover you only have $475.

PayPal now allows for Credit Card processing without forcing buyers to create a PayPal accounts. All they need to do is enter their card details and a purchase can be made. This is good news, because it removes one more obstacle from the mantra of making it as easy as possible for people to give you money.

Generally, PayPal seems to work. It takes little effort to set up an account, and I recommend (with some reservations) that you do so. If you don't want to chance doing business with PayPal, you'll need to accept that you're cutting off a not-insignificant avenue for revenue. There are alternatives to PayPal: `moneybookers.com`, `yowcow.com`, and `clickbank.com`. Each has its own quirks.

Credit Cards

This is the grand-daddy of payment methods. If you want to be serious about collecting revenue from your audience, you *must* endeavor to offer credit cards as a method of payment, no ifs, ands, or buts.

A major drawback to offering credit cards is paperwork. You'll often need to have a merchant account, which means you'll need a business account at a bank and, therefore, you'll need to operate as an actual company. The details of starting up a corporation or proprietorship or partnership are beyond the scope of this book, but there are plenty of references available out there.

Assuming you have all of the correct pieces in place, you'll now need to find a credit card processor to handle the transactions; you can also rely on PayPal's new Credit Card service, but the rates you'll pay are often higher. A multitude of such services exist out there, although two I can recommend in the U.S. are PayByWeb.com and CardService.Com. One I can recommend for Canada is Beanstream.com, which is the processor I use for UF.

Credit cards, like PayPal, actually cost you money. As an example, most processors will ding you a monthly fee of between $15 and $25, plus a percentage (2.5 percent to as high as 8 percent) of each transaction.

Before you sign up for credit card processing, make absolutely certain you understand their TOS and how they operate chargebacks. What would be ideal is a processor that doesn't allow for chargebacks for services or virtual items, although this is quite difficult to find. At the very least, you should be aware of what you could be exposed to and plan accordingly. If your membership fees aren't high (say, $10 a year), a couple of chargebacks a month probably won't be much of an issue to you. If you charge $5,000 a year for each Super Platinum VIP Membership and you get only one or two of those a year, someone who charges back that amount can really hurt you financially, especially if it's after you've shipped the goods.

A No Refunds clause in your TOS can protect you legally should you decide to launch a lawsuit to recover the funds in a chargeback. Be sure to carefully balance the funds lost against the value of your time, energy, and public relations. Sometimes it's just not worth going after someone for the money.

For what it's worth, in the years since I started selling memberships at UF, I have never had a single chargeback.

Maintaining Value

So, now you have your paid memberships available, you're promoting some tangibles and intangibles as a reward for paying members, you offer checks, PayPal, and credit cards, and you're running news items and ads on your site to make your audience aware of your offer. The money starts to roll in and you're busy with fulfillment. What next?

Having all of this set up isn't the end of it, not by far. Selling memberships is a constantly evolving thing, and a moving target. If you constantly offer the exact same tangibles eventually everyone in your audience who is interested in buying a membership won't want to renew because they already have those goodies. Mix it up! Change the art or the items at least once a year. Come up with something unusual and you'll spark some interest. There are so many possibilities that listing them all would fill a book on its own.

Just to get you started, visit Branders at `http://www.branders.com/` — it's a premium branding company. Its business is putting people's logos and artwork on items ranging from clothing to pens to balloons to watches and binoculars. For a brief time, I offered Dust Puppy Antenna Balls at UF, and they were a smash hit. I dropped them from the lineup after discovering how difficult (and expensive!) they were to mail in envelopes. Most of the items I ship to paying members are flat, so adding something like antenna balls was really kind of stupid.

One thing you should do when you're collecting information from people who buy a membership is make certain you get a working e-mail address. Assure them that you'll never spam them (and don't lie about this — if you spam your audience even once you will strip-mine any trust they had in you) and that the e-mail address was just so that you can e-mail them a reminder when their membership is a week away from expiring. I've learned that people actually want a reminder, and consider it a valuable service.

Finally, re-examine your pricing schedule every year. As you add features and content to your site, there's a good argument to be made for increasing the price of memberships. UF will have completed its eighth year in November of 2005 — that's eight years of daily cartoons, almost *3,000 cartoon strips* all in all, available to be read in the archives. Once you've built up a sizeable collection of content that people can enjoy, you're well within your rights to ask for a few dollars more from your audience to support your efforts.

chapter

To Gate or Not to Gate

The dearer a thing is, the cheaper as a general rule we sell it.

— *Samuel Butler*

I f you're reading this book, I'd wager that you're probably not a multimillionaire. You might be working toward that kind of financial status (and with your talent and the business guidelines in this book, I hope you get there!) but people who need business guidance generally aren't what the financial community calls "High Net Worth Individuals." I also recognize that I could be quite wrong, that there could be a millionaire out there reading this book right now with a mind to selling his or her creativity on the Net. If so, just be aware that some of the following may or may not resonate with you.

Life in a Gated Community

The question of gating off part or most of your site is best answered by your own attitudes toward life in a community. Have you ever driven or walked through one of those expensive gated communities that have their own uniformed security and fences everywhere, not to mention pools, tennis clubs, golf courses, and a plethora of other fine luxuries? Most likely, you've only ever driven by one — entry requires that you be a resident or an invited guest.

People who live in gated communities are attracted to them for a couple of major reasons: The first and most obvious reason is *security*. They perceive that the security provided by the fancy gates and walls and security officers will keep crime at bay. Once past the gates, they're in their castle, and it is well-defended by men-at-arms. This reason has little or no bearing on the online question.

The second reason, and perhaps the most compelling, is that of *exclusivity* (there it is again). People who live in gated communities find value in being one of a small number who can afford to do so. It's all part and parcel of feeling like one belongs to a special club that not just anyone can join.

The same kind of psychology exists to a significant extent within online communities and audiences. There is certainly a fraction of any given audience that is attracted to the idea that they're one of a special number. Unlike the real world, however, this fraction decreases when money is involved. Online community members seem to prize exclusivity more when it has to be earned in some way or granted through a vehicle that is not a commercial transaction.

Gating Off Your Site

So, should you gate off part of or all of your site? If you like exclusive communities with small audiences, the answer is probably "yes." If you're more interested in deriving as much profit as possible, the answer isn't so clear-cut.

Let's consider the central issue and the likely results. If you make all of your content available for free, and do not gate off any part of your site, you will maximize the size of your audience. This will, in turn, give you the most pageviews and, therefore, most banner impressions to sell. You will also incur the most cost in bandwidth, assuming your traffic breaches your monthly allotment.

If you gate off part of your available content (and there are a few ways you can do this), you will reduce the size of your audience. This means fewer pageviews and fewer saleable banner impressions but also lower bandwidth costs. Also, assuming that your content has enough demand, you'll generate some revenue from people who pay to access the gated content.

Anyone with even a shallow background in business will understand that there's a min-max graph involved here where you're trying to figure out what combination of gating and free content would generate the most revenue. Unless you have a business analyst working for you, I recommend you take the easy way out: do it all or nothing, with a lot more weight to making it all free.

There are very practical reasons for this. Unless you're already an established content provider, few people are going to risk even $1.95 a month to access content they know little about from an author they know even less about. At the beginning, you need to encourage your audience to grow, and nothing attracts people to a site more than access to something they enjoy at no cost to them.

Once you're established, you can change the rules of the game a little. However, beware that gating off access to part of your content will be met with at least some backlash. Remember that in any audience you'll have a bell-curve of personality types and value systems, and the extreme ends of that curve are never going to be happy with any changes you might implement. Changes that deny your audience access to your hard work without some kind of contribution will, without a doubt, cause at least a few of them to write and inform you of your shortcomings as an author. Take it in stride. Creating and sharing content as a career or sideshow will teach you how to do this with hard experience over the years.

So, given that you've decided to gate off one or more sections, you'll have to decide *what* to gate off. Here are a few possibilities that might work for you:

1. *Gate off your archives* — If you produce, for example, a daily column or cartoon strip, over time you'll have built up a considerable archive. UserFriendly (UF) has as of this writing close to eight years' worth of daily cartoon strips. If you visit ucomics.com, you'll notice that it gates off cartoon strips other than the last two weeks. If you want access to the entire archive, you have to pay. This method is very compelling, but keep in mind that this also destroys your largest base of page (and, therefore, banner) impressions. People love to go back through archives and they do it more than once.

2. *Gate off your current content* — This flips the previous method on its head. Rather than gating off the archives, you make it so that the latest two weeks' worth of content is accessible to paying subscribers only. Some people are willing to wait the 14 days to see what you wrote or created, but a lot of people are driven by what is considered immediately topical.

3. *Gate off the whole site* — I really don't recommend this one, because it relies on your ability to promote and sell your content to potential audience members with just a few samples of your work. You might be very good at this, but most content creators aren't advertising geniuses. Be careful if you go this route; you could easily demolish your entire audience base if you don't handle it correctly.

4. *Gate off a second content thread* — This one is more compelling than Number 1, because you're continuing to give your audience free access to your original content, and you're offering up further original content that no one else has seen before accessible only to those who pay. Those who love your work are much more likely to pay for an intangible if it happens to be content you created.

Some of the big online newspapers and journals do a variation of Number 4. They give readers access to part of the newspaper (say, a third of the stories), making sure that there are a couple of big headliners in there. The rest of the newspaper (notably its columnists and opinion pieces, both of which command a faithful audience) is available for a fee.

Note the key icon next to some of the articles in Figure 4-1, from the *Globe and Mail*, arguably Canada's leading newspaper. All articles that are so labeled are gated off and are available only to those who pay for access. Clicking on the article leads you to a page that urges you to buy a membership to what the *Globe and Mail* calls the "Insider Edition," as shown in Figure 4-2.

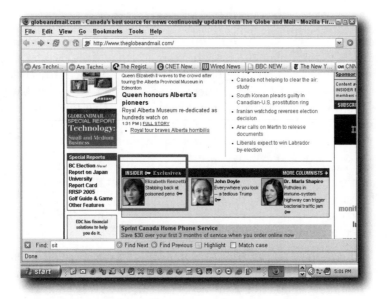

FIGURE 4-1: *Globe and Mail*

The newspaper also makes it a point to showcase all of the benefits of paying for access. As you can see on its "Insider Edition Tour," shown in Figure 4-3, you not only gain access to the locked-off articles; you get a customizable home page at the *Globe and Mail*, top business news from the *Wall Street Journal*, access to a dedicated news ticker, and some other interesting features.

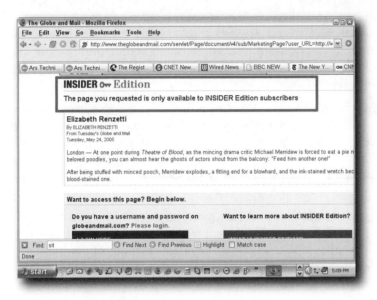

FIGURE 4-2: "Insider Edition"

FIGURE 4-3: Insider Edition Tour

What the *Globe and Mail* also does that is clever is offer people a 14-day free trial. It asks for your information and a credit card number, then gives you access to the site for two weeks. If you don't notify them to cancel your account before those two weeks are up, you're charged for a membership and you're a member of their "Insider Edition" club.

Asking for financial information does two things: It scares away the people who aren't serious about wanting the content, and it gives you (as a content provider) a better chance at closing a deal with a subscriber. Unfortunately, it also tends to give pause to people who are semi-serious about buying your content. It's par for the course, however. People still have some difficulty with paying even paltry amounts for content on the Net.

Remember that you don't have to charge money for access to gated content. You could exact a different sort of payment from those who desire access to the vaunted, exclusive areas of your site. Non-payment methods of passing the gate aren't as simple to resolve or track, but the end results may be more valuable to you than the cash you could normally earn. Following are some ideas:

- *Audience members are required to earn a certain number of "points" before they can enter the gated zones* — These points are earned for posting in your forums; the more they interact and post, the more points they earn. The forum software PHPBB (`http://www.phpbb.com`) has a module called the "Cash Mod" that automatically awards and keeps track of a user's points. Once a user has earned a specified number of points, the user can trade them in for access to the gated part of your site. You could expire the access after a period of time, which motivates your users to continue posting and interacting so they can afford the points to buy access again when theirs expires. The benefit here is more potential pageviews as users refresh forum pages and click to read posts.

- *Grant access for a period of time to audience members who voluntarily view an ad, as per Salon.com's SitePass program* — The beauty of this method is that it drives up the value of your ad impressions because viewers are "opting in" to view the advertising. "Banner blindness" is far less of an issue if the ad takes up the entire page and can't be interrupted with a click. Salon.com usually runs Rich Media ads in this manner with full flash animation and sound. Once the ad finishes running, the viewer is sent on to the gated content, which the user can peruse for the fixed period of time (in Salon's case, it's for the calendar day).

- *Points can also be awarded to users who spread the word about your site* — A registration system that keeps track of recommendations would be required. When a new reader signs up for an account on your site, he or she enters the username of the reader who recommended them. Once a certain number of referrals are signed up because of that reader, he or she is granted access to your gated section. You'll need to make the sign-up procedure thorough for this to minimize abuse and faked referrals. Asking for a real e-mail address, phone number, and half a page of info is usually enough to deter most casual scammers. The benefit here is building a larger registered audience base using your readers' personal social networks.

- *An ad hoc award system whereby you award exceptional contributions by your readers manually* — The amount you award is entirely by your own fiat. Contributions could include fan sites, strange but impactful advertising for your site (a UF fan once wore a Dust Puppy t-shirt when she entered a wet t-shirt contest!) or anything you consider helpful. Once a user has reached a point total, he or she is granted access to the gated portion of your site. Although the benefits are obvious, the nature of awarding points manually and by fiat can be very time-consuming. You don't want to end up penniless and in ill health like H.P. Lovecraft, who spent more time writing long replies to his fans than he did writing stories.

Cash Poor and Intelligence Rich

Something we haven't discussed yet is the value of cash-poor but intelligence-rich audiences. (This isn't to say cash-rich audiences are necessarily intelligence-poor!) Many of your audience members will likely be people who live paycheck-to-paycheck, or are students, or may even be retired. The best of this group are people who want very much to support you in what you do, but who simply can't afford any luxuries in their lives. I used to be a university student, and if I had to choose between having Ramen to eat versus a paid membership on a Web site, even a Web site that is beloved, the salty carbohydrates would win out.

This particular slice of the demographic pie is driven by two things: appreciation of your work and, unfortunately, guilt over not being able to support you financially. It is critical that you never lose sight of the fact that businesses don't succeed on money alone! These people are the ones you particularly want to listen to, because most of them will substitute ideas and volunteer efforts for money.

There is something to be said for creating a special "class" or "rank" of audience member, one that cannot be bought with money, only earned through volunteerism. That rank might be given limited or even full access to the gated part of your site via a point system as described previously. Additionally, you might want to grant them access to their *own additional* exclusive part of the site, making it a special point of recognition for anyone who has earned your gratitude with hard work.

Given that you will eventually attract enough audience members who want to help you thrive, you should make it a point to help them do this. Create and give them a "kit" of promotional material they can download and distribute. Although there will be as many different kit designs as there are sites, I recommend that you provide them both online and offline materials. Online material might be just a collection of half a dozen banner ads and tiles of the most popular sizes. Offline materials should be something along the lines of an Acrobat PDF file of a letter-sized poster (A4 for Europe and Australasia) that can be easily printed off and posted up in an office or on a billboard. Provide a color version as well as a grayscale version. You might as well give your fans the option of running off full-color posters if they want to.

If you'd like more ideas, head over to http://www.moneyforcontent.com/ and you'll see some example promotional kits that might inspire you.

The "quality" of your audience is undeniably affected by your gating policies. It is arguable that a pay-only audience will be made up of people who have a more-than-casual investment in your work and your site. This can help raise the caliber of discussions in your forums, an issue that is fairly serious when it comes to attracting more of the same. I'll discuss community behavior policies in Chapter 6.

The argument on the other side of the coin is just as valid, however. Audiences who pay for access also feel more entitlement to your content and use of your site than ones who do not. Someone who has money to spend isn't necessarily more likely to be an upstanding community citizen than someone who doesn't have the money but is socially invested in your forum. In fact, an argument could be made that people who pay for access could potentially abuse their exclusive status by lording it over other audience members, and if you attempt to enforce civility, they may be the most difficult to deal with because you engaged in a commercial transaction with them.

It should also be noted that having a large paid-subscriber base makes your site even more attractive to advertisers. They view the paying members as people who love your content enough to pay for it. This is somewhat ironic because many paying members give you their money to view your site *without* the ads.

So, where does this leave you? Ultimately, you're in the same place as you were before you read this chapter, but now you're aware of most of the more common results and effects of choosing gated versus ungated content. I maintain that gating off content is a bad idea at the beginning, but could be lucrative once you're established. You'll have to gauge your own audience in this, something you'll be quite practiced at doing by the time this question rears its head.

chapter

5

Branding and Merchandising

Whassssssuuuuup?

— *From Budweiser's 'True' ad spot, written by DDB.*

In 2000, *Globe and Mail* columnist Naomi Klein released a seminal book on branding called *No Logo* that uncovered the machinations of the North American corporate sector under the auspices of a branding culture. The book wasn't at all flattering to the corporations that were scrutinized by Klein's fiercely perceptive and analytical eye, and it served to reveal a lot of the treachery that is being practiced on consumers by the owners of the most powerful brands in the world today.

Having said that, branding in and of itself isn't an evil force. In fact, it can be one of the most useful tools in your business arsenal. What's important is that you don't use your brand as a cloak for shady practices, as is explained in Klein's book.

The concept of branding as central corporate gospel really took hold in North America in the 1980s. Prior to this, corporations were about making things in factories and on assembly lines. People bought North American products because they were made in North America. Although a company's brand was considered important, it still took a back seat to the business of *production*.

By the mid-1980s, a few bright management theorists pushed forward the notion that *making* things was a far more troublesome road to riches than marketing things. Large companies that produce things are responsible for factories, thousands of employees, and all of the bureaucratic apparatus that goes with production operations. But factories with workers overseas that you could contract were cheaper and involved less risk. Your overhead would drop, and you could spend all of your time pushing your brand out into the world, making claims of superiority via implication and clever advertising. People would buy products *with your brand on them* because you've convinced them that your products are better, or that anyone who buys your products has impeccable taste. It didn't matter that the products were made in Thailand or India, or even that your competitor's products were made in the same factory. It soon became all about who had the better, more recognizable, more fashionable brand.

It's important that you understand advertising and branding are not the same thing. Branding is a much larger concept; advertising is merely a subset or part of a branding plan. (Sponsorships and logo design are other parts, for example.) Naomi Klein offers an excellent explanation: "Think of the brand as the core meaning of the modern corporation, and of the advertisement as one vehicle used to convey that meaning to the world."

The "core meaning" of a corporation, then, is the "soul" or cultural value offering of that corporation. Coca-Cola, for example, is the drink of the everyman, and if you drink Coke you're someone who, at one point in Coke's advertising life, would like to "teach the world to sing in perfect harmony." In other words, Coca-Cola associated itself with peaceful, friendly, and humanistic values. This is Coca-Cola's brand, or core meaning.

Branding came about almost naturally at the turn of the twentieth century. The decades prior saw advertising tasked mostly to inform consumers of all of the new inventions that were available on the market. Prior to the invention of the light bulb, everyone used oil lamps. Advertising had to not only tell consumers that the light bulb was available; it had to convince them it was better than the oil lamp.

There was very little going on in the way of branding at that point. People were more concerned about whether to buy a telephone, not what brand of telephone to buy. Some token attempts were made to promote "Smith's Goods" over "Jones' Products," but for the most part, consumers were just interested in getting their hands on (or resisting the urge to buy) the latest improvement that would help better their standard of living.

Then along came mass production thanks to the assembly-line factory. The market was flooded with items that were pretty much the same across the board, and this is when branding began to really shine. You have to remember that prior to mass production, people would go to their local retailers and buy soap, flour, and rice out of the barrel regardless of brand because it was the same product no matter who supplied it. The shopkeeper would be an advocate for products, and consumers would generally buy what the shopkeeper recommended.

With the advent of hundreds of similar products (and they were similar to the point of being almost exactly the same once you got the wrapping off), there had to be a way to differentiate between them — or so the company men thought. As far as the consumer was concerned, buying the same bar of soap was just fine.

So, the company men went to the ad men and asked for help in branding. Thus was born advertising that began associating products with lifestyles, values, and personal identity. You could indeed continue using Mr. Gable Jones' Soap, but if you used Frog Hollow's Oat'n'Milk Soap instead, you'd not only be clean, but you'd be a wholesome, virtuous person, too!

Over the following century, branding grew into a force. By the 1980s and 1990s, it was all about the brand. Ads convinced you that your computer just wasn't up to snuff unless you had "Intel Inside." People were debating over the virtues of Pepsi versus Coke, but everyone knew that Coke was "it." Nike urged North Americans to "Just Do It." We aren't being informed; we're being assaulted with value judgments.

You Are Your Brand

Here is where the idea of branding can be useful to you, the creator. When you write, play, draw, or otherwise produce something, that creation is your expression. Your creation is a reflection of who you are at that moment, and it has the marks of your essence as a creator upon it. What this effectively means is that anything you create is branded by what is distinct about you.

Consider what it is that your creations communicate over a longer period. The stories told within your content aren't as important as the subtextual message that is always there when someone consumes your work. Leo LaPorte and Patrick Norton of *The Screen Savers* (and now *This Week In Tech*) have established a brand that is distinctly theirs: a fun, chatty, interesting show about computer technology that is stamped with their personalities and the chemistry they share as co-hosts. This is why when *The Screen Savers* was cancelled they had no problem rebuilding their audience with the *This Week In Tech* podcast — their fans value the "Laporte & Norton" brand over the name of a show. When you listen to Leo and Patrick do their thing, you know that they're providing you with quality information, all done under the auspices of good humor and a very enjoyable rapport with their audience.

Anything you create will have its own qualities and subtext. It's a wise thing to pay attention to what that subtext is and whether or not it's the brand message you want to telegraph to your audience. Are you meticulous or anal? Professional or amateurish? A deconstructionist or a builder? Do you take issues surrounding your chosen art seriously or glibly? All of these questions answer themselves eventually as the qualities of who you are as a creator and the work you do emerges.

In a lot of ways, your brand is your "face" on the Net. Even if you travel to conferences, it's doubtful you'll ever meet more than 5 percent of your audience in person, and even that's an optimistic percentage. People who visit your site and take in your work will unconsciously form an opinion of your character and that of your creation by the qualities you imply. If you promise to update your content every day of the week and miss a few days here and there and it becomes a bit of a pattern, you can bet that people will consider you to be flaky and not terribly reliable. And it doesn't matter that those times when you missed an update you had serious emergencies! Remember that on the Net, people base how they view others on far less information than they would normally in Realspace.

At this point, you must ask yourself a few questions. When you come up with the answers, try to keep them down to a single sentence at most and a single word at best. Brands that are the most effective (for both the brander and the consumer) are the simplest both in concept and expression. "Coke is it" is such a simple, powerful idea that everyone "knows" that Coca-Cola is the leading cola product, even if they prefer Pepsi or Dr Pepper.

(As an interesting aside, Coke today is thriving very well on being a nostalgic brand, and now stands for 1950s Americana. Although it no longer enjoys sitting at the peak of iconic culture, a recent bright spot occurred when it brought back its classic Coke bottle design by reshaping plastic bottles to mimic the glass. Coke's 1950s myth returned for those who could remember the little glass bottles.)

Following are the questions you must ponder to come up with a solid brand message:

- How am I trying to present myself (and my work) to the world?
- What is the central quality of my work?
- Who am I to my audience?

For the sake of spring boarding your own thinking on this, I'll give you my own answers based on what I do at UF:

- *How am I trying to present myself and my work to the world?* — Professional and connected
- *What is the central quality of my work?* — Insightful
- *Who am I to my audience?* — A trusted commentator

This exercise brings to the forefront who you are and what you're trying to do as a creator. This is your brand, the qualities that you have detailed in your answers.

Keep in mind that your brand is also something that you're constantly striving toward. You might find being insightful on a daily basis is a piece of cake, but you still need to stay on target, or you're changing the nature of what you present to the audience. This is bad because you're confusing what you're about as a creator. If the central quality of your work is "unpredictability," that's fine, but don't start being predictable!

This is a common problem faced by all companies that use branding as an important component of their business strategy. Once you've committed to a branding concept, you have to walk a bit of a tightrope to remain on message. If you fall away from that message, it can take months (if not years) to effectively re-assert the old message, if not a new one. When brand is all you have that differentiates you from the competition, it's crucial.

Thankfully, you won't have quite the same problem as the big corporations. Changes in your branding message aren't expensive unless they're negative, destructive transformations. Consumers like stability in the brands in which they invest, so working hard to stay on message is a good practice.

By the way, an important element of every brand is the logo. Make sure you have one and be certain that you're happy with it. Re-branding your logo can be an expensive and time-consuming, particularly if your audience has grown accustomed to the previous one. If you have design skills, put them to work. If you don't, I recommend you do what the guys at *This Week In Tech* did: they asked their audience to send them some suggestions and were overwhelmed with the number of submissions. No matter how many (or how few) logo suggestions you receive, remember that you can only use one. Keep in mind as well that the most successful logos are ones that work in print as well as they do on the Web. Simple, bold designs work the best. Think Nike, Apple, and Mercedes-Benz.

Now that you have your brand figured out and you're using it as a compass to keep you on course, you'll be in a good position to use it to earn revenue. As you'll see, this thought exercise does have a real-world purpose.

Leveraging Your Brand with Endorsements

Cultivating trust in your audience can be one of the most useful and powerful ways to leverage your brand. It takes time (often years), but once you have an audience's trust, it can really help with your bottom line. Keep in mind, however, that it only takes a few seconds to completely strip-mine that trust. Don't ever risk it if you rely on your audience's faith in you to earn money. It's also a question of ethics.

An *endorsement* is defined as an explicit approval or sanctioning of a commercial product or service. The only time this really matters to the consumer base is if someone famous (or notorious) makes the endorsement. The celebrity is putting his or her reputation behind the product or service. Clearly this is done at some real risk, because if the endorsed item is less than adequate, that celebrity isn't going to have much ability to promote other items at a later date. Think about Suzanne Somers and that ghastly Thighmaster contraption. Not only does it not help you lose weight, it's moderately dangerous if you're a man. Although Somers looks great for her age, anyone who gives it any thought realizes that she remains in top shape thanks to expensive personal trainers and a workout regimen that covers quite a bit more than what is effectively a thigh-sized nutcracker.

As an online content creator, you'll be a celebrity in your own circle. Your fans will certainly consider you to be someone at least quasi-famous, and will — once your brand is out there and you've earned their trust — pay attention to any recommendations or endorsements you might make regarding products and services. Because creation is a personal affair, your audience will feel like they know you and will trust what you have to say. As mentioned before, any abuse of this trust is done at considerable risk.

A multitude of services and products are available on the Web, and they're all fighting for eyeballs. They all want to get in front of *your* audience (and everyone else's) because of the direct relationship between the number of people who browse their products and the revenue they make. You may receive a lot of offers, but I wager that most of them will be affiliate deals, and you know how I feel about those.

But one day a company will contact you and they'll have a product or service you find you can really get behind. Maybe it's a software package you've used for years, or a brand of motor oil that you already recommend to all of your friends. Whatever it is, it strikes a chord with you because you already consider it to be something of great quality.

Alternatively, you might be the one contacting the vendor. Perhaps you've used an off-site data storage facility for a few years and found its service to be truly superlative. You've established a rapport with the vice president of marketing and feel that it's time to approach him or her with a proposal. Either way, the situation you're in is one where you'll be trading your brand's endorsement for money.

When you endorse something, you're telling the audience that you and everything you represent (as conveyed in your brand message) supports that product or service. In fact, you're implying that *that product or service is of a high enough quality to be equal to your brand*. Not only are you approving this product or service, but you're also staking your reputation on its quality. Your audience will implicitly understand this.

Most any company would love an endorsement from someone who can influence potential customers. Endorsements require little work or effort on their part — they simply utilize the influence and watch the sales come in. An endorsement from you, however, isn't just a risk to your reputation, it also impacts your ability to endorse products or services in the same category.

For example, I heartily endorse and recommend Register4Less as a domain name provider. The deal it offers is solid and cost-effective, and the people running the company are highly ethical, a very important consideration for myself because trust is an important part of my own brand. However, because I endorse Register4Less, I'd have a hard time effectively endorsing another domain name provider. Most of my audience would be confused and wouldn't know which one to choose. In fact, it would probably reduce the effectiveness of my first endorsement, and that wouldn't make anyone happy.

To avoid this, and to encourage companies to obtain an endorsement from you, I recommend that you build in exclusivity as part of the endorsement package. When I endorse a company's product or service, that category is locked out. Register4Less will be the only domain name provider I'll endorse and even let advertise on UF. It makes endorsements more effective, less complicated, and overall more pleasant.

Endorsements must be long-term, at least 12 months in length! The vendor benefits from this by being associated with your brand for long enough to really sink into peoples' minds. If a vendor were to bail on you after 3 months, you have to wait for your endorsement of that vendor to fade from your audience's memory before you can effectively endorse another vendor in that category. This loses you months of potential revenue. Make absolutely certain that any endorsement deals you sign are for a period of at least a year, and there should be no "out" clauses that allow the sponsor to terminate early without payment of the entire sponsorship. Be sure to give *yourself* an escape clause that covers your interests should the sponsor do something that harms the reputation of your brand by association.

A typical endorsement deal doesn't exist. They can be anything you want them to be. The one UF has with Register4Less involves a monthly payment from Register4Less. In return, they receive at least one prominent tile on the home page, a certain number of banner ads per month, access to the UF audience for focus groups (more on these in Chapter 6), use of the UF characters in promotional material, and my explicit blessing and endorsement made public. They can use my endorsement anywhere they like, although it has the most impact, for obvious reasons, on the UF Web site.

Before you make any endorsement deal, be sure of two things: that you really, honestly do love the product or service and that you're getting something fair for your end of the deal. Endorsements are the most "expensive" form of promotion you can sell, because it's your reputation that is on the line. This shouldn't be simply given away, nor should you discount it. Like any deal, it has to be fair and attractive to your client, but don't forget your side! You probably won't be able to make many endorsements in your life (nor should you, because you devalue your endorsements if you do too many), so doling them out carefully is a good idea.

Your Art Promoting Your Art

One of the more difficult aspects of earning a living as a content provider is extending your reach beyond the pond that is yours. If you do good work, you can count on a certain amount of traffic to reach your site simply through word-of-mouth. Most of this will come from online communications, including e-mail and mentions in blogs and other content sites.

But then there's Realspace. There aren't too many people who can afford to rent a city billboard, much less pay for the cost of design and production work for something to put on the billboard. Nor can the vast majority of us afford television or radio commercials. We're too poor to get rich the way the rich stay that way.

Someone in the mists of branding history came up with a shockingly good idea: *vendorwear*. This is simply a t-shirt, polo shirt, cap, or other apparel that has blazoned upon it the company's logo. These are often given away (you might have to give them your personal info that they can use in market studies) to people at conferences. Few people would turn down a decent-quality bit of clothing that would normally run them $10 or $15 at the store. If it had on it a logo of a company that was deemed cool at the time, so much the better.

When done in large enough production runs, a company might pay $4 or $5 a shirt, tops. At the larger conferences you can expect attendances in excess of a million people, so if you plan appropriately it's unlikely you'll have too many shirts to hand out. For the sake of example, let's assume that our company bought 2,000 t-shirts at $5 each. For $10,000 then, the company is able to hand out 2,000 t-shirts branded with its logo and collect 2,000 data records for its marketing department. Potentially, our company will see 2,000 people walking the halls of the conference advertising the company's brand for them! How many pairs of eyes will fall onto this logo? How many people will through repetitive exposure begin to think about this company in the backs of their heads? Ten grand is a very small portion of any large firm's annual marketing budget. The Return On Investment (ROI) in this endeavor is generally very good.

This phenomenon of *vendorwear* can help you as well. Your audience comes to you because they value the content you provide, because they trust in your brand. Those who are interested in buying apparel with your brand's logo, or artwork, or whatever it is that identifies your work are not only paying you for branded merchandise, but they're advertising your brand for free every time they wear the shirt or hat and go out!

The entire concept behind wearing branded clothing really took off thanks to the Tommy Hilfigers and Calvin Kleins of the world. Many people really do choose their clothing because of the brand — if you don't believe this, you can watch it in action at the dealers room at a comics convention. Watch people browsing a shirt rack choose between a t-shirt with a Batman logo on it versus, say, a shirt with Spiderman art. I'd bet that the t-shirts are close enough in quality to not make a difference, yet Spiderman fans aren't going to opt for a Batman shirt. Fans are consumers; they have simply bought in to the Spiderman or Batman "brand" instead of Banana Republic or Abercrombie & Fitch.

There's no reason why people can't eventually buy into your brand the same way. Of course, you have to give them the opportunity.

Jurassic Park Had it Right

Remember when the first *Jurassic Park* movie was released how it was accompanied by a veritable flood of *Jurassic Park*–branded merchandise? You could buy shirts, jackets, hats, plush toys. . . the list was impressive. People love dinosaurs, so it was easy to see why *Jurassic Park* in all of its original endeavors did so well.

I'm not suggesting that you do the same as the *Jurassic Park* people did. For starters it's highly unlikely you have the resources they did, and ordering shiploads of merchandise in hopes of selling it all is a sure way to financial suicide. But in the beginning, it wouldn't be such a bad idea to at least make a high-quality t-shirt or hat available to your audiences, emblazoned with your brand, of course.

I mentioned high-quality for a reason. If your brand represents nothing else, it should always be associated with quality goods. There aren't many things more disheartening than to see your brand into which you've put countless hours of blood, sweat, and tears stamped on a t-shirt that looks like it belongs on a 99-cent clearance rack. Always aim for the better-quality item.

The psychology behind merchandise quality is a sound one. People are already paying a premium for a t-shirt with your brand on it; most of them won't object to paying a dollar or three more for a t-shirt that is top-quality over an average one. Most of them will thank you for it.

When you're shopping around for a merchandise supplier, you should stick to one rule: *always ask to see a sample before committing to anything*. If the merchandiser inveigles, move on to a competitor. There is no substitute for having a sample shirt, hat, or antenna ball in your hands to touch and examine. The last thing you want to have happen is for a merchandiser to ship you 50 t-shirts that would make great dishrags, especially after you've paid for them. Take no chances with your money or your brand!

I learned this rule the hard way. At one point, I asked a merchandiser with whom I had done a great deal of business to create a UF-branded foam-covered bat. This was the realization of a storyline I wrote that involved a mythical "Big Foam Cluebat." A lot of my readers wrote in asking me to have the bats made and offered for sale, a good indication that sales of the product would be solid.

Because prior merchandising efforts (including shirts, pajamas, hats, plush dolls, posters, and so on) went off very well and always with high-quality products, I asked the merchandiser to proceed with the sourcing of the bats and then the sale of them. This was a mistake.

It turns out that the merchandiser misunderstood me. I had wanted bats that were like the foam-covered kiddie baseball bats, the ones with the rigid core. They thought I wanted a piece of foam that was cut into the shape of a baseball bat. The end result was a piece of floppy foam with the words "Big Foam Cluebat" stamped on it. When I received one, my heart sank.

It sank even further when I discovered that more than 200 of them had already been sold and shipped. My readers bought the bats relying on my reputation and my brand. I was on the cliff's edge of a disaster that would erode my brand with at least 200 people, and likely many more as news spread about the less-than-adequate foam bats.

I did the only thing I could at this point if I were to save my brand's integrity. I contacted the merchandiser, instructed them to pull the bats, and to give everyone who had bought a bat their money back. This ended up costing me a not-inconsiderable amount of money, but I believe it would've cost me much, much more in the long run if I hadn't done this. In the end, I did more good for my reputation than I could've expected.

Traditional Merchandisers

The traditional merchandiser is the ideal partner in your quest to spread your identity and message through branded gear. Their *raison d'etre* is the creation of branded merchandise, and they make a lot of their money by offering "full service fulfillment," a term that means they do everything from production to packaging to shipping. You simply provide them with the artwork and any specifics you have regarding the design. They take it from there, either shipping out according to a list you give them, or directly selling items for you to your fans.

Depending on the structure of the agreement, you'll either be their client or their licensor. If you're a *client*, you just have them produce the goods and ship them to you. You pay for them up front and make your money back as you sell items. This is the least-favorable kind of deal for independent content providers because it means tying up your money in inventory that sits at your home or in storage somewhere. Also, if you go this route, your business has changed from providing content to being a merchandiser. The last thing you need is something that detracts from your focus. I don't recommend you go down this path unless you have the considerable resources required to pull both businesses off successfully and concurrently.

As an aside, if you do have the ability to handle fulfillment, you can make pretty good revenues provided you have the marketing and audience to back it up. The business of merchandising deserves its own book, so if you want to explore that option, I suggest you refer to existing materials on the topic.

If you're their *licensor*, you're in a great position! This means you've granted them a license to produce goods with your brand on them, and in return you receive a royalty on goods sold. Generally, you work with them on deciding what should be going onto the goods and the sort of items to be branded. After that point, they take over, although you're likely expected to promote the items on your Web site.

You'll be paid a royalty, and this number can vary. It's usually a single digit, say 5 percent to 9 percent, but some of the more successful content providers can command 10 percent or more on a deal. The percentage also depends on whether you're paid on *wholesale* or *retail*. Wholesale prices are what a merchandiser would charge if they were shipping a volume of your goods to a retailer elsewhere. It's usually 15 percent to 40 percent less than the retail price. You'll get a higher royalty percentage if you're paid on wholesale. Being paid by *retail* is fairly common nowadays, although most royalty percentages will hover no higher than the 5 percent mark.

As a licensor, you'll need to negotiate what privileges the merchandiser (as the licensee) has and specifically exclude what you don't want them to have. This is an excellent occasion to retain a good Intellectual Property lawyer because you're effectively signing over commercial rights to someone else. Commonly, a merchandiser will want exclusivity so they're not competing with other merchandisers. Agree to this only if they're able to produce everything you want them to do. No sense in being stuck with someone who can only do hats if you want to offer shirts to your audience.

Also, they'll want either an out clause or a very long term with no performance guarantees. You can agree to the out clause provided they can't invoke it until a certain amount of time has passed. Remember the risk of endorsement? Your audience won't appreciate it if you switch merchandisers every three months. Insist on a 24-month contract with a 30-day out clause after 12 months that either of you can invoke. Don't agree to long terms with no performance guarantees. In fact, perhaps you can state within the contract that they must produce x new items every month or every three months for sale, just to keep the choices fresh. It also gives you a bit of guarantee that they're actually trying to sell items with your brand on them. If they fail to do so, they'll be in breach of contract and you'll be able to cancel the license.

On-Demand Merchandisers

You do have another choice that doesn't involve a full-service merchandiser. On-demand merchandisers such as `CafePress.com` and `Zazzle.com` are companies that specialize in only producing items as they are ordered. Instead of them or you sitting on inventory and tying up cash, companies such as these only produce branded items as people order them. If someone orders three t-shirts, only three t-shirts are branded and shipped.

Both companies allow you to create personalized "online stores" with all of your items grouped together on a Web page. Buyers will use the CafePress or Zazzle shopping cart and merchant account. Once sales of your items exceeds a certain amount (usually $25, or more, if you set it higher), the company will send you a check.

This method is very attractive to the small business, but it has its drawbacks. Generally, items sold through CafePress or Zazzle are quite a bit more expensive than those bought from full-service merchandisers. This is part and parcel of having very small (and, therefore, labor-intensive) production runs. Also, the quality of the items may not match that of the full-service shop. CafePress offers a wide range of products you can brand (from mugs to bibs to shirts), but the method of transferring the art is similar to using inkjet transfers you can buy at an office supply store. Zazzle uses a higher-quality transfer process, but its selection of items that can be branded is very limited: shirts, cards, and posters as of this writing.

Nevertheless, one of these companies (or one like them) is often the best bet for small content providers looking to get their feet wet in the merchandising game. CafePress offers a "mark-up" payment scheme. They tell you how much they charge for an item when it's sold, and you mark it up as you see fit. For example, every standard t-shirt CafePress sells goes for $12. If you mark it up to $14, you get $2 for every t-shirt that your audience buys from CafePress with your brand on it. If you want, you could leave it with no mark-up, thereby giving CafePress all of the profit. However, if you're offering your art or brand for sale on items to merely raise awareness, keeping the price low may not be such a terrible idea.

Zazzle offers a royalty scheme, one that is based on the retail value of an item. Contributors (those who provide the artwork) get 10 percent, while referrers (people who send buyers to Zazzle through their Web site, like an affiliate deal) get 7 percent. If you set up your own store at Zazzle and refer people to buy items with your artwork or brand on them, you get a whopping 17 percent of the sale.

Something to bear in mind with on-demand outfits is that most of them charge higher-than-usual shipping and handling costs. I don't doubt that they figure this into their revenue models because it's easier to sell someone on a $15 shirt with $5 shipping and handling tacked on instead of an $18 shirt with $2 shipping and handling added. Unfortunately, there's no way around this other than finding a competitor that doesn't charge high prices on either the item or on shipping.

chapter

6

Online Communities and Online Consumers

The Seven Commandments are abridged for the last time, simply reading,

"All animals are equal but some animals are more equal than others."

—Animal Farm, by George Orwell

When the Web began the climb up the hockey stick curve of popularity, the mantra was "build it and they will come," referring to the phenomenon of huge washes of traffic appearing at sites where there was at least minimal content. But this was in the beginning, when the Webscape was relatively sparse. Nowadays, sites have to fight for traffic, and do everything they can so that they'll be noticed. Given the huge sea of sites out there, stumbling across a particular one — say, yours — quasi-randomly is about as likely as finding a particular drop of water in a bathtub in the dark.

So, "build it and they will come" is no longer true. This goes double for online communities. Ever since the halcyon days of the late 1990s, companies and individuals believed that as long as they provide the means for community discourse on the Web, a community will sprout. A significant percentage of people continue to believe this constantly growing falsehood.

Despite all of this, a loyal community has become one of the most valuable derived assets a site owner could have. As time passes and the Web matures, business concerns that ignore the power of online communities do so at some considerable risk. If nothing else, they'll be losing out on a priceless source of market feedback and a potential consumer base.

Online communities (or just "communities") are not consumer bases, but the two groups have considerable overlap. A *consumer base* is explicitly a group of people who are potential buyers of a given service or product. These people are also qualified as buyers who not only have the resources to make a purchase, but are *more likely to spend money on said service or product* than the rest of the general public.

A *community*, on the other hand, is a group of people who share common interests. "Share" is the key word here. Ten million people who enjoy the writings of H.P. Lovecraft who don't communicate with one another can hardly be called a community. Sharing and participation are critical elements of any online community's success. If everyone sat back and refused to put forth questions and offer ideas to their peers, there'd be no reason to bring them together in the first place.

Consumer Culture Versus Community

The consumer today is driven by three factors: convenience, price, and brand. As long as a product or service excels in two of the three factors, it's likely the product or service will do well. The value system of the consumer revolves around the question "what do I get for my money?" The "what" can include speed of delivery, how convenient it is for the consumer to make the purchase in the first place, the quality of the goods or service, and the like. All of these elements add up to what retail experts call "the customer experience." If the "experience" is acceptable for the money being spent, the consumer will be inclined to complete the transaction.

The value system of an online community member centers around a much larger, more complex question: "Do I belong here?" Belonging, as psychologists have told us for decades, is one of the most potent motivational forces in the human psyche. Its power comes from a primal need for acceptance in the tribe; banishment usually meant the loss of security and a very real increase in risk of death.

No one is going to die if they're banished from an online community, but anyone who invests themselves into a community of any sort is going to feel the pangs of rejection if they're ostracized. For this reason, many of the principles that govern human behavior in Realspace communities are applicable to non-Realspace ones. This includes the value of a community as a responsive consumer base. Communities, as you will see, offer many valuable elements that simple consumer bases do not.

Communities: Realspace, Online, Distributed

Ever since the advent of the Bulletin Board System (BBS), online communities have taken their place beside the much older and more mature Realspace communities. There is one additional community type that has evolved that deserves mention: the distributed community. These are online communities that encourage face-to-face Realspace meetings between its members. Although much of the communication between such members remains online, any relationships they share are enriched by physical gatherings. It is arguable that the evolution of an online community into a distributed one is a sign of good health.

The differences between online communities and real-world ones have been studied extensively by social scientists. Understanding these differences (and the important similarities) helps us make smarter decisions on how we, as content providers, should relate to our audiences.

Consider this:

> *"Historically, physical proximity has been a necessary condition for intensive human interaction, and, thus, has been a key aspect of a traditional community. When we aspire to define, observe or construct other types of communities, this seminal concept tends to frame our perceptions. Our use of the term 'Realspace' to denote a non-digital community is one example of how pervasive this impact is.*

> *"Specific communities of interest typically develop within a larger community based on the shared needs and desires of a subgroup within the larger community. Conversely, a geographically based community will seek to communicate its needs and desires beyond its physical boundaries. By developing the mechanisms that allow them to do so, they are able to form larger communities of interest. Communities of interest are not dependent on 'Realspace' or physical geography, but rather are dependent on a human geography that takes into account the shared needs, desires, and ambitions of its members.*

> *"It's also important not to dismiss the role played by the implementation of technologies. Whether it's been a transition from clay tablets to papyrus, Guttenberg's printing press, the telegraph, or the frenetic growth of the Internet, the development and dissemination of technologies that foster social interaction have always had an impact on the development of communities of interest. It's an impact that can easily be overlooked in favor of the concepts, ideas, dreams, and desires that a medium communicates.*

"I see online communities as an outgrowth or evolution of more traditionally conceptualized communities of interest. I use the term Electronic Community of Interest (ECI) to differentiate between digitally dependent online communities and those communities of interest that augment their traditional presence with online technologies. ECIs are dependent on this emergent form of communication for their success, but in general, they are eager to explore the myriad possibilities it offers. Just as there are a multitude of 'Realspace' communities of interest, there are many different forms of ECIs. In my experience, there are five significant functional differences between an ECI and either a Realspace or traditional community of interest: scale, accessibility, the democratization of knowledge, the ability to utilize both synchronous and asynchronous communication modalities, and the ability to consciously design and engineer the rules and norms for social behavior.

"The Internet provides an opportunity for anyone with access to communicate with like-interested people around the globe. Never before in the history of humankind has the average individual had the ability to interact with others on such a scale. If one seeks to develop an ECI, the potential to reach and communicate with like-interested individuals is far greater — and is possible with far fewer resources — than has ever been possible before.

"In Realspace, everyone can listen, but not everyone can be heard. On the Internet, the communication process is more accessible. Everyone can listen, speak, and find the motivation to act — not only as an individual, but also collectively as part of a group. The interactive nature of this communication differentiates the Internet from other technologies — historically, it has become easier to broadcast or disseminate information (think newspapers, radio, and television) — but the Web allows individuals to participate. Rather than being passive consumers of information, they react, respond, and reframe information as knowledge. An ECI provides the structure and framework — the 'space' — in which to do so.

"In very general terms, traditional communities have primarily relied on synchronous communication (conversations and other 'real time' forms of interpersonal interaction) and on the asynchronous dissemination of information (printed materials, telegraph, radio, and television) that lack an interactive component. The online community changes all of that. You can (and do) have both. Synchronous online communication is similar to face-to-face or telephone interaction in that it occurs in real-time. No big difference there, except for the ability to do so with nearly anyone on the planet. However, the ability to communicate (as opposed to disseminate) asynchronously

with people—either individuals or groups—is highly significant. You don't have to figure out the time zone changes or the cost for a transatlantic phone call in order to communicate with a friend in Switzerland. You simply post. They can read and reply when it's convenient for them. The asynchronous nature also allows the communication to be shared with others at a later date. The ubiquitous 'threads' of shared, Web-enabled communication are not only woven across time zones, but across time itself.

"Generally speaking, this shared knowledge is more accessible because the Internet is less restricted by social mores and institutionalized authority than any other form of community. This freedom provides the opportunity for a community organizer or content provider to consciously develop the social structure and framework— the boundaries, social mores, norms, and expectations—of an ECI. It's important that this framework evolves dynamically, but the core structure can be created by design."

— *Mark "dire lobo" Suazo, sociologist and member of* UserFriendly.Org

The Ivory Tower: A Nice Place to Visit, but Living There?

The infamous *Ivory Tower* is where people go when they like to remain above the unwashed (and even washed) masses. Some academics, many creators, even more celebrities, and most politicians have keys to the place, not to mention entire suites of rooms of their own. A lot of people who reside there do so out of choice. Some live there because they were put there and they don't know how to get out.

The ones who were put there are victims of circumstance. When the gatekeepers controlled the only game in town, a lot of creators were only reachable through their keepers, whether they were syndicates, record labels, or their public relations firm. Layers upon layers of screening kept the creator or artist apart from his or her fan base. Creators heard only the good news, and fans received only boilerplate replies. This wasn't necessarily a purposeful exile instituted by the gatekeepers. Before the Internet, communication channels tended to be restrictive and/or slow.

The Internet opened up a huge bypass, and now fans can write or even speak directly to their favorite content providers. Now it's a simple matter for a content provider to engage in dialogue with his or her fan base. This dialogue isn't restricted to what the content provider's ego may want to hear either. Being blunt or even tactless over the Net carries far less social risk than if the same thoughts were communicated in person, as shown in Figure 6-1.

FIGURE 6-1: Punched in face UF cartoon

Online communities don't automatically dismantle Ivory Towers. Content providers could easily enable their audience to reach one another, but by keeping their e-mail address obscured and choosing to put filters in place (human and otherwise) they can still lock themselves away from their fans. Pertinent, desirable e-mails can be forwarded by a staff member. Online forums don't have to be read.

However, there is a very compelling business case to be made for not only connecting to your audience, but becoming an integral part of the community that surrounds your creation or content. It should be obvious that any business can benefit from having intimate, detailed knowledge of what its customer base thinks. The trick is in translating this knowledge into useful data, and making the most productive decision possible.

When an audience member writes in to express an opinion or concern, this is simply anecdotal evidence. Receiving 500 such e-mails and observing a corresponding event (such as a drop or rise in readership) may indicate you're seeing empirical evidence. Either example is data, but one is obviously more accurate (and, therefore, more useful) than the other.

So, how should you treat this potential trickle or flood of information from your audience? A simple rule to follow is to *never, ever ignore a constructive comment.* This doesn't mean you have to take some action in response to every e-mail that expresses a dissenting opinion about your work. Rather, you should prepare to adopt a larger perspective and place the comments you receive in that context.

Every audience in existence will suffer from the inherent properties of a bell curve. The bulk of your audience will likely be made up of moderates, people who enjoy what you do to a varying extent and who remain relatively silent. On the ends of that curve, you are guaranteed to find extremists of both stripes: people who blindly believe you can do no wrong and their diametric opposites, people who refuse to acknowledge you can do anything right.

To use a subcultural vernacular, by the very nature of the extreme, you'll feel that the ones shouting the loudest are the flake-boys (and girls) in your audience. After absorbing e-mail from your readers over a period of several months you'll come to the not-unreasonable conclusion that you're either a content god or you're sewer filth, and it's quite possible you'll think you're both. The truth, as is usually the case, is somewhere in the middle, this I assure you.

Content, particularly original, artistic content, can only be viewed subjectively. Some people love and adore Mozart. Some people hate, hate, hate his work. The man was a genius, but even he has his detractors. On the same note, artists who drop bricks on live rodents as a form of "art" have their devotees. My subjectivity in the last two sentences is not only obvious but unavoidable from where I sit.

This is something you'll need to take to heart as a content provider. On the Web, the risk of immediacy from proximity is absent, so critiques will be that much harsher and often expressed with more condescension. My advice is to keep it in perspective; the opinion of one (or even a few dozen) people matters little when your audience numbers in the thousands or millions. You might also want to feel amused over the idea that someone could possibly invest that much vitriol and emotion in an e-mail sent to someone who provides them free content. Free content that, I'd like to add, they don't have to consume.

The key assumption here is that you're not charging for content. If you do, you might want to take any critiques a little more seriously. But if a reader spews bile at you, I'd suggest discounting their remarks and offering them at least a partial refund. If they hate what you create so much, it would be better for both of you to go your separate ways.

Given that dialogues between the content provider and his or her audience and between audience members themselves can be frankly honest, what does that mean for you in a business perspective? Quite simply, your community becomes your looking-glass. Major corporations spend tens of millions of dollars every year in market research and analysis to uncover the best way to extract money from their consumer base. An online community offers you the same opportunities in a microcosm, but with a built-in safety valve. There is nothing evil about trade, but there is something evil about exploitation. Your safety valve is found in your community's feedback, a system that gives you an immediate measure of business and content decisions you make. Being a small entity gives you an advantage over the big guys — you can turn on a dime if your community gives you indications that you're off your moral compass.

This, in a nutshell, is why you should never reside in *Chateau d'Ivory*. The people who enjoy your work have invested themselves in it and would like to continue doing so. Thus, if you do something they feel isn't "right," they'll take the time to let you know. Pay attention when they do! They're freely providing you information from a consumer's perspective — information that the Microsofts, General Motors, and IKEAs of the world pay large fortunes for.

(Think of it in terms of llamas. You're the head llama, and you have a herd of other llamas following you around. If you don't do your job as head llama, several (or many) llamas will come up and spit at you until you do better. Some llamas will just quietly leave. One thing that can't happen is a llama taking your spot as head llama in your domain. At most, they'll set up their own llama range and attract their own herd.)

Assuming you've grokked the value of a community of your own, one of the most obvious uses for such a community is the formation of impromptu focus groups. Market analysts hold these in Realspace to collect opinions and feedback on projects that are either under way or being considered. The differences are in your favor — you don't need to rent a meeting room, a projector, or advertise for volunteers. All you need to do is post your questions on your forum, or invite selected members to join a private mailing list and ask your questions there. In fact, an electronic discussion may give better results because the participants have more time to consider their answers.

In short: Stay out of the Ivory Tower, enable the formation of a community, and become an integral part of it. Your business may never reach its true potential if you don't.

Shared Thoughts, Shared Experiences, Shared Reviews

Perhaps the most compelling basis for communication between people is that of sharing. We socialize mostly to belong to a tribe, whether it's the Geek Tribe, the Single-Malt-Scotch Tribe, or the Good-Heavens-Isn't-Diane-Lane-Hot Tribe. Obviously, our efforts in socialization are rewarded most in tribes where we share common values and interests, and, thus, we find ourselves gravitating to groups where we feel we most belong.

Online communities allow anyone with a Net connection to socialize, even the most socially disabled introvert. This is because we can derive some social rewards by simply reading what others have written; reading a post and thinking, "Yes, I totally agree with her (or him)" validates your own position at no social risk to you. Simply knowing that people that think like you do exist and are reachable by e-mail is a powerfully validating bit of information. There is comfort in knowing that you aren't entirely alone.

Given that online "tribes" form strong, validating connections between its members, you can bet that any information of note that one of them receives will be disseminated very rapidly to all of the other members. It doesn't matter if some of them live in Detroit and others live in Vladivostok. The Net and the social networks that have formed on top of it guarantee that rumors, information, and gossip will spread at the speed of typing.

This means that online communities possessing strong internal bonds have become the equivalent of niche consumer interest groups! You can bet that UF's community members advise each other on technology purchases with a frankness that gives marketers the chills. If something really sucks, they'll say so. What can be so damning is that a lot of my audience members are alpha geeks and/or highly accomplished experts in their chosen fields. The last thing a company like, say, Cisco would like to see is a distinguished network engineer give a new Cisco router the thumbs-down in widely read public forum. The UF forum is read by tens if not hundreds of thousands of people per day, many of them influencers of technology purchases at big companies.

The Web empowers the smaller forums as well. Even if you only have an audience of a couple thousand people, they do have the ability to spread what they learn from other community members across the Web with links. Not everyone limits themselves to a single forum, and one individual can spread a bad review across many pertinent audiences.

This is the power of a true online community — sharing important information.

So That's What Mayors (Are Supposed to) Do

Exactly what is an online community and how does one begin? For starters, online communities are different from "audiences." An *audience* is a passive, one-way consumer group. They read, watch, listen to, or somehow consume the content you create. They may interact with you via e-mail or other channels, but that is the extent of their reach.

Communities are audiences that not only interact with the content provider, but also with *each other*. This is known as *many-to-many interaction*. Once the process of socialization begins, you have the spark needed for the formation of a healthy, growing community. You also have something that will soon become a chaotic mess that could implode on itself if it's not managed correctly.

Referring back to the "build it and they will come" mantra, it's important that you disabuse yourself of this notion. Setting up forum software and calling it the "Clever People Forum" is not going to attract clever people (or any people at all for that matter) to your site, nor is it going to persuade them to start interacting with one another once you get them there. This truth will come as a crushing blow to most people who have never been part of an online community before.

Getting such a beast going requires two specific elements: an *initiator* and a *maintainer*. The initiator can be anything that attracts people to your site: a daily cartoon, editorials, podcasts, music, any service or product. Ultimately, it must be something that generates enough interest in potential visitors to compel them to take the time to load up your Web page. Additionally, they have to know that your site exists in the first place. Keep in mind, though, that even if everyone is aware of your site, if it has no compelling content no one is going to bother visiting.

The *maintainer* is what keeps people coming back to your site, and it needn't be just one thing. It could be exactly the same thing as the initiator — for example, the UF daily cartoon serves both functions. Or, you may have more than one maintainer, as in UF's case where there is both the cartoon strip and the forum. The forum not only enables the community to share ideas in a common space, but the friendships (and more!) that have formed there draw people back on a regular basis.

Luckily for most content providers, the content we provide usually serves in both capacities. A daily cartoon is no different than a daily blog entry or a podcast in this regard. It's also a very good idea to offer more than one maintainer, and an online forum makes for an excellent addition. Enabling this kind of interaction on your Web site can mean more pageviews, a "stickier" site (marketeer lingo for a site in which visitors spend more time), and an overall more compelling experience for the audience. Setting up forum software is fairly trivial, and the rewards can be remarkable.

Running a forum as the mayor requires you to be many things: psychologist, sociologist, constable, judge, diplomat, and tyrant, just to name a few. What's more, you have to be perceptive in each of these roles. It's very easy to become heavy-handed in your role as your forum's constable, for example. It's also easy to be too forgiving in the same role. A happy medium is a tightrope — be prepared to fall off many times as you learn how to manage your forum membership.

I make the assumption that you want an orderly, well-maintained community that doesn't run amok. Once you have a steady flow of repeat traffic coming to your site, and once some of that traffic engages themselves in your forum, unless you set a precedent it is almost a law of nature that the discussions will rapidly deteriorate and become generally immature, uncreative, and most of all unproductive. I liken this to a clean, pure stream in parkland. The campers who show up will, unless encouraged by precedent that is enforced by regulations, eventually sully the stream and render it into a channel of sewage.

This occurs partly because there are few convenient and immediate social consequences for behaving like a dork on the Web. It's not just the 12-year-olds acting like 6-year-olds with an uncreative handle on foul language. You'll also find 40-year-olds behaving like they're monkeys flinging poo. When you can be anonymous and have few or no consequences governing your behavior, it's easy to let slip the ego and id and show the worst elements in your personality.

Many, many examples of this can be found on the Web, and naming a few would be an injustice (some don't deserve the attention, and others are fine sites if it weren't for the community). Instead, I'll offer a couple of examples of online content sites that have healthy, constructive online communities.

Ars Technica (arstechnica.com) is a PC enthusiast's news site that offers often insightful commentary on that latest in PC technology. It covers a wide gamut of topics, including (but not limited to) games, hardware, applications, and science. The site community initiator is the commentary offered by knowledgeable writers who are themselves PC technology enthusiasts. Community members discuss both the news item and the commentary offered. The to-and-fro that goes on is of a consistently high caliber, although there have been a few cases where the usually excellent debates have deteriorated into name-calling and he-said she-said shouting matches.

RPGnet (rpg.net) is a role-playing gamer enthusiast's news and review site that covers the world of both face-to-face and computer role-playing gaming. It has a lively community whose members share their opinions of game (and ancillary) products with each other. The debates tend to be in some ways just as technical as the ones you'd find on Ars Technica; they also can be enlightening or banal.

In both cases, the community members are really quite involved with each other and the site, clearly investing themselves in their efforts to communicate. And you'll note that even though they're both successful, they have their share of problems. This is part and parcel of running a community online and something you'll not only have to accept, it's something you'll also have to expect.

Understanding that there are social difficulties (and strengths!) inherent in online communities will go a long way toward preparing you for forum leadership. Once again I turned to a trained professional for insight:

> *"The initial reaction of social scientists and other pundits commenting on the rise of digital communication and the advent of ECIs was a somewhat pessimistic assumption that it would be difficult (if not impossible), for individuals to develop significant, substantive relationships in a virtual world. As Katz and Aspden summarized, this was essentially 'speculation that Internet communication alters cultural processes by changing the basis of social identity, thereby displacing the socially grounded identities of everyday synchronous discourse.' Although this perspective is rooted in a number of theoretical constructs (even a postmodernist approach), I believe that it was shaped more by a mindset that 'community' is rooted in physical rather than human geography — and as noted, this assumption has obvious limitations.*

> *"Similar arguments have been made regarding the negative impact of technological innovations on social interaction since the advent of the telegraph. That's not to say that there aren't significant difficulties in creating an online atmosphere which fosters involvement, interaction, and communal relationships. The lack of physical proximity does shape an ECI — no matter how warm an Internet 'hug' is, it will never replace the physical act.*

> *"This reaction was rapidly countered by the position that online interaction was totally positive, and would reshape the world into a better place. Mitch Kapo (founder of Lotus Development Corporation and an advocate of Open Source technology) is such a proponent. In 1993, he wrote that 'Life in cyberspace seems to*

be shaping up exactly like Thomas Jefferson would have wanted: founded on the primacy of individual liberty and a commitment to pluralism, diversity, and community.' Despite the growth ECIs as agents devoted to fostering social or political change (think MoveOn.org*) and Mitch's more recent ponderings that 'Tom Paine would be writing Common Sense on his Linux box today,' the truth can be found by blending these extreme views.*

"Proponents of both positions have typically relied on highly intelligent and well-meaning arguments backed by anecdotes and examples, rather than data concerning the growth and development of such norm-based communities and their impact on Realspace communal interaction.

"There is a growing body of research that indicates that online interaction can be significant, substantive and even therapeutic. Much of this research focuses on health or medical related ECIs, and the support and validation one can receive via the Web has proven invaluable to many individuals. There is a saying that a problem shared is a problem solved, and an ECI allows its constituents to do so in as openly or anonymously a manner as the individual is comfortable with. One rationale for this efficacy is that the pool of potential 'problem resolvers' and 'commiserators' is so vast. Another is the diversity of experiences and cultural perspectives that the constituents bring to bear. It has been said that by acting in locum tenentes for psychotherapists, physicians, lawyers, programmers, or other professionals, ECI constituents have come to the aid of many people who either lack the resources to access to one in Realspace, or who would be uncomfortable participating in a more intimate, face-to-face setting. I believe that the nature of this interaction can be considered a real strength of ECIs. This also illustrates another strength of online communities — the ability to find information that may not otherwise be readily available. This democratization of knowledge is one of the key aspects that the irrepressible Web optimists latch onto as a sign that the Web will change social interaction and community involvement as we have traditionally conceived it. I have no doubt that it has — and will continue to do so — but there are other factors that limit such.

"From the standpoint of a content provider, one of the most difficult aspects of fostering an online community is overcoming the signal-to-noise ratio. In order for a nascent community can be recognized as a destination worth traveling to, it is critical to stand out among the oft times overwhelming amount of information that flows on the Web. Whether it's a support group for people with a specific health issue, a presence that allows professionals to communicate and collaborate with colleagues, or publishing a daily Web cartoon, finding and exploiting a niche or area of interest which individuals have an interest in isn't enough to make an ECI successful.

"Compelling content provides the locus for 'visits' and 'page views' but unless it fosters a shared discourse and encourages an emotional investment, it will probably lack the inertia or vitality required to fully develop. Whether you choose to call it a 'marketing plan' or 'outreach and education,' implementing a mechanism to make the ECI recognizable and inviting to those who could have an interest is critical. Otherwise, it's just another tree falling in a forest full of falling trees — and it can't be heard over the noise.

"One of the most significant aspects of participation in an online community is the ability to create alternative personas. As with many of the characteristics of an ECI, this is both an inherent strength and a danger. One only has to scan the mass media for examples of 'Internet predators' who take advantage of this characteristic.

"Depending on the community, there may be a fairly large percentage of active participants who consciously develop such a persona for far less devious reasons — oftentimes it is simply a desire to maintain their anonymity.

"However, recent studies indicate that despite the use of a 'handles' or nicknames, active participants — those who engage in such norm-based communities over time — cannot help but allow their personality and values to become apparent. In short, if you choose to invest the time and energy to become a community member, the real 'you' eventually emerges. Other constituents may not know your real name, but they know the real you."

— Mark "dire lobo" Suazo, sociologist and member of `UserFriendly.Org`

Given that there are inherent pitfalls in online community building, that a percentage of your visitors are going to invest less in the community than you'd like, thus allowing themselves to act destructively, what should you do? How do you handle "conduct unbecoming"?

Conduct Unbecoming, or "Everyone Behave!"

It would be really nice if you could just assume that all of your forum participants will simply act like mature, intelligent adults. Unfortunately, it's unlikely that all of your participants are going to be adults, and even worse, a lot of adults have a real hard time clinging to any semblance of civil discourse when the threat of Realspace consequences is removed from the equation. The assumption you thus logically have to make is that people won't behave. People are selfish. People can be real dorks.

We do have a solution for this in Realspace: the social contract. This is a set of rules, both written and unwritten, that you and everyone else are expected to obey. If you don't obey the rules, there are consequences. Simply knowing that this social contract exists tickles our need for tribal acceptance (as we are for the most part social creatures) and solves a lot of immediate behavior problems.

There is an important psychology and ethic behind making your social contract clear. Assuming you have the ability to lock accounts and ban IP addresses (and most Content Management Systems and forums do), it's critical that your participants know what constitutes punishable behavior on your forum. If they don't know, it'd be like living under the rule of a schizophrenic. You don't know if you're going to be banned from one day to the next, and this makes it difficult for anyone to want to invest themselves in your forum and the community.

An explicit social contract — in other words, your set of laws — gives participants a sense of security in two ways: first, they know that others will abide by these laws or face punishment, and second, they know that doing X won't get them banned, but doing Y will. Both make it safer to invest yourself into the community online. Rules are useful. Just make sure they're easy to access and are available to all to read.

But how do you go about defining what that social contract is? What kinds of policies should you have in place? What actually works and is fair?

- *Write a central policy that is geared for your audience.* Enforcing a policy that doesn't allow freedom of dissent on a site that purports to uphold free political discussion is going to cause only people who like the current government to gravitate to your forum. In other words, figure out what is the thing you most want to promote and base your central policy on that. For example, at UF, I above all prize the civil exchange of ideas. My central policy reflects this.

- *Decide on the maturity level you wish to attract.* This will determine what kind of language and topics you will allow. As a writer, I use swear words sparingly, but I do recognize them as useful tools at times. On the Net, however, if you allow swearing at all in your forums, you can expect the language level in debates to plummet rapidly. (This is where having a "no *ad hominems*" rule — no personal attacks in debates — can help maintain some quality in your more heated forum discussions.) Sometimes it helps to consider what film rating you'd like to be awarded for the content in your forum (and perhaps your site overall). I've pegged UF at the PG level; some mature themes, but generally the language is kept at a level that encourages some of the younger kids to drop by. More to the point, it encourages their parents to *allow* them to come by.

- *Determine punishment scales ahead of time.* For example, what infraction would cause instant IP banning even if it's the first offense? What are minor offenses, and are there different punishments (say accounts locked for different periods of time) for first, second, and subsequent offenses? What if someone offends repeatedly—at what point do you ban them entirely? For the record, anyone who posts illegal material or links to illegal material on UF is instantly banned and their information is handed over to the authorities. As a site owner, I can't take the risk of someone encouraging the swapping of warez on my forum, because angry companies with much deeper pockets than I could wipe me off the map with their lawyers. Consider this sort of thing carefully.

- *Be absolutely certain that your central policy is worded as simply and clearly as possible.* And vague isn't necessarily bad! UF's central policy is "Don't make the forum a bad place." This sweeping edict covers so many possibilities that if someone does something that is harmful to the community, but isn't covered in a specific sub-rule, I can still take action. This particular blade is double-edged, however. Because it covers so many possibilities, some forum members can feel a bit persecuted if they keep doing the wrong thing, unsure of what is acceptable. It's a constant struggle, so think about your central policy at length. Also, make it clear that members who skirt the line don't get a free pass. This isn't a court of law, it's a forum owned by a private person who has to pay the bandwidth and hosting bills. The *spirit* of the law, not the *letter*, is what holds reign.

A logistical issue is that unless you care to read through your entire forum from top to bottom every day, you might want to consider appointing a few trusted souls as moderators to assist you in enforcing policy and helping the newcomers with the rules. The best moderators are the ones who don't participate in discussions much, because this allows them to remain aloof and as objective as is reasonable. If a moderator does get involved in a heated debate and things start getting out of hand, make sure that a *different* moderator resolves any issues. Unless you want your team of moderators viewed as members of a junta, it's a good idea to keep any conflict-of-interest out of the picture.

Forum policies should be seen as an organic part of the greater whole that is the community. This means that you should be prepared to change the policy as your audience changes, or if you see the policy failing in some way. Keep in mind that you needn't make policy entirely in a vacuum. It's often helpful to have your moderators examine a new policy and give you feedback. Your forum members could come up with the most useful and insightful comments of all. There is something to be said for putting a policy out to public discussion because it's always good to have it examined from all sides. Pay attention to what your members have to say, but make it clear that you reserve the right to make the final decision. Online forums seem to work best as benevolent dictatorships, not pure democracies.

Even the most reasonable policy doesn't protect you from the one thing you can never control: the vagaries of human behavior. I put the question to UF's chief moderator — a volunteer who has helped me shape forum policy from the early days — regarding the pitfalls of community policing:

> *"Prigs and Punks. While having a great technical system for managing the community will help considerably, the problems the community moderator will encounter are all human-interaction problems and someone who creates a community needs to understand that. Knowing the audience will help to tailor the rules of the community, but no community I've ever encountered has an audience that fits the initial expectations of the creator of that community exactly. Because of that, the members of the group will create interactions with each other that will surprise (astound, in some cases) the moderator and all the members of the group that do fit into the initial mold that the community was created for.*
>
> *"The best example of the Prig I've seen was on a Zen Buddhist mailing list, where the group generally was focused on very peaceful interactions, as you'd expect. One participant though used the forum to expound on the failings of previous teachers in a very aggressive way not in keeping with the usual interactions between members. While the creator of the community and all of the 'regulars' wanted to be inclusive and shape this person into a form that would work, in the end that just wasn't possible. Not everyone who joins the community (even when the community is invite-only) is going to be the right shape to fit into the jigsaw puzzle. In this case, that person didn't have a purposeful intent on destroying the community, though she was not overly concerned if she did. That's a Prig.*
>
> *"Punks are a lot different, because not only do they have the lack of concern that the Prig does, but actively want to disrupt, destroy, or otherwise create problems in the community. These are the people that the rules are made for and these are the people who will actively seek holes in the rules that they can exploit to say, 'You can't touch me, I didn't break any of your laws'. In the anonymity of the Internet, these Punks believe that they are invulnerable deities of 'their' domain, and their domain encompasses anywhere they choose to interact with other people. In a sociopathic sense, the Punks don't even really absorb the fact that other people in these communities exist. They are playthings no better than intelligent robots. The Punk will actively usurp authority and attempt to tweak the nose of the moderators at every opportunity.*

"As for technical pitfalls, the creator and moderators need to have the tools to police the community effectively. In Internet terms, that means locking them out, either temporarily or permanently. In systems that require non-immediate registration for participation, locking the user's account for a time period in direct relation to the seriousness of the offense is the only real tool available. An enterprising user (likely a Punk) can switch IP addresses and be back causing havoc quickly, but a process for account creation that is non-immediate will cause most of these to disappear. A 15-minute turnaround on this is wonderful; when someone is choosing to cause problems for entertainment, boredom is your greatest weapon."

— *Greg "Kickstart" Webster, Chief Moderator at* `UserFriendly.Org`

I also asked Greg for his advice on policy creation. As my site's Chief Moderator, he doesn't have the luxury of being the site owner (with all of the dictatorial powers that accompany such), nor that of being a line moderator who can simply claim that he was doing as he was asked to by the policy-makers.

"Look for loopholes. In reality, any policy that is too rigid will ultimately fail. The 'Don't make the board a worse place' rule at `UserFriendly.org` *is a great general rule that can be called on to remove Prigs and Punks alike. A policy that, for example, listed all of the 'forbidden' words will just result in people finding new words that are just as offensive, but aren't forbidden and, therefore, can be 'rule-lawyered'.*

"Knowing the community also means accepting community input on the rules that are made. Not everything should be up for an Athenian democratic vote; the moderator/creator of the community needs to decide the overall direction the community must take. However, the community should be consulted on additional rules that fall under the scope of 'daily operation' once those basic groundrules are set.

"Finally, as much as I am a bad example of this, don't create permanent policy on the fly. A single-day rule that stops a bad situation is fine, but creating a far-reaching policy change based on a single circumstance in an established community will rarely be supported or successful."

— *Greg "Kickstart" Webster, Chief Moderator at* `UserFriendly.Org`

UF's online forum has evolved dramatically over the past few years. We have a mature central policy and several sub-policies. The punishment scale currently in place seems to work well for the given audience. I have the good fortune of having several level-headed and perceptive volunteer moderators from several different time-zones helping me keep an eye on the forum. Above all, I have an audience that has, for the most part, been an absolute joy to work for.

Loyal Communities = Happy Customers

It all comes down to treating your audience and forum members with respect, and giving them the ability to share common interests with one another. This has the useful side effect of connecting you directly to them, and giving them a place to air both their concerns and compliments. Remaining accessible to your audience not only earns you their respect, but gives you every reason in the world to remain true to your original vision that you have sold to your fans. This leads to a customer base that will remain with you over the long term, as you show them that you consider their opinions not only material, but critical.

Because the opinions of my own fans are of paramount importance to me, I only felt it was appropriate to poll one of them for his opinion on the entire question of finding success in online communities. You already have perspectives from both a professional sociologist and an experienced moderator. To close off this chapter, I offer you an answer from a forum participant's point of view:

"First, and foremost, is a requirement for respect among the community members. The expression 'netiquette' has been coined to describe socially acceptable behavior when participating in on-line activities. Essentially, 'netiquette' boils down to being polite when addressing others, showing due respect for opinions posted in earnest, and generally just acting like a mature human being. Some fluff often gets tossed in about using proper grammar and spelling, but that is simply a matter of form, not of substance. The 'signal-to-noise ratio' in on-line communities is not so much a matter of how easily one may extract meaning from any particular contributor's posts, but rather of how much meaning is there to be extracted. Humans grow up learning to hear intonations, to see facial expressions, postures, and gestures, and to gain information from all kinds of cues that simply do not exist in virtual space. The words one offers on-line are the sum and totality of the message one is presenting. HTML and RTF can make those words livelier, and emoticons and blocking can enrich the words, but the words are all there are. So, addressing people respectfully, using kind words, and thinking about what one is typing become much more important in an on-line community than spoken words are among friends seated around a table together. There is nothing other than those typed characters to show that one actually values the input of others.

"Given that one's words become critically important when on-line, it behooves one to avoid casually, or even deliberately, tossing out words meant simply to deride or belittle. Such words only cause annoyance and don't really contribute anything more to a discussion than would the words 'I disagree.' Or perhaps even 'I strongly disagree.' Such a simple statement can be read, noted, and even challenged if some other member of the community feels it is worthwhile. Thus, the discussion can progress. But, anything in excess of a simple disagreement that says nothing more than actual disagreement, is noise. It is meaningless and bothersome to those who read it, searching for a bit of signal amidst all the diatribe. And it can be avoided merely by being respectful, even of those with whom one disagrees most vehemently.

"The UserFriendly community (aka "the Ufieverse") sums it up very well with their prime directive: 'Do not make the board a worse place to be.' They also publish a set of rules for behavior on the board in their FAQ. Every one of the rules, and every decision of how to enforce those rules, is derived from and governed by that prime directive. One could argue that 'worse' is an extremely subjective term, but, in the end, such argument is moot. Contributors are not held accountable before a court of law, where the legal standards must be precise and free of ambiguity. Rather, they are held accountable to the community to which they are contributing. Such is necessarily inherent in the nature of on-line communities.

"Every on-line community has its own unique feel, and its own specific rules of netiquette to which all of the members of that community mutually subscribe. One violates those rules at the risk of becoming outcast by the other members of that community. Actual expulsion, by losing one's access privileges, is usually after the fact of social ostracism directed toward a member who persists in being 'noisy' by consistently or flagrantly violating the community's standards. Not surprisingly, this is the case in all human communities; it is not unique to virtual space. But it becomes highlighted in virtual space due to the essentially anarchic nature of the Internet. There is no, and can be no, single governing body in virtual space; every on-line community is autonomous and sovereign within the space of its own servers. Therefore, community standards become much more inescapable on-line than they seem in the 'real world.' With no body of law to which one can appeal, and no due process for appeal, it is the community standards of the sites one visits that completely govern the acceptance of one's behavior.

"To return to the point: A successful community is one where the rules of netiquette intrinsically support the dissemination of meaning among the contributors. Generally, this is accomplished by compelling a respectful attitude, quelling abusive behavior toward others, and allowing community members to be whatever they like to be while they are on-line.

"Notice that the above does not require a member to be 'on topic'. Topicality is a community standard of some on-line gatherings, but the communities I find most interesting and enjoyable are those where contributors can offer their thoughts on just about anything under the sun, and a few other things besides, too. By and large, those who participate in these forums are a very imaginative and creative bunch. And it's quite fun to see what such quick and agile minds can come up with, when let free to do so.

"Success is a tricky recipe — a brew of respect, seasoned quite spicily with freedom to express oneself, and kept only at a rolling boil with the ability to enforce the netiquette of the community."

— *Shawn "Bitflipper" Bean, UF member*

chapter

in this chapter

☑ Consumption Junction

☑ Discontent over Content

The Ethics of Creation and Consumption

The creditor hath a better memory than the debtor.

—*James Howell, c. 1594-1666*

Human beings expect things of one another. The expectations of others are usually learned because they tend to be implicit instead of explicit. Many of these implicit expectations are put there by social contract.

On occasion, you'll run across a situation where that social contract isn't followed by all participants. This means that some members of a given group don't agree with the contract that you understand, and, therefore, reject your position. In the world of the online content provider, this often means that the reader blocks your advertising and yet continues to cheerfully consume your work.

This can be a little disturbing, especially given the rapacious nature of a large percentage of the contract-rejectors. A common behavior found among them is the aggregation of all of their favorite content under RSS or on a Web page that is built by their own scripts on a daily basis. Is this theft? That's a hard one to answer.

Before I delve into the ethics of the matter, let's have a look at an implied contract I use at UF. Having been written and essentially codified, the contract isn't really implicit anymore, although some would argue otherwise. I'll cover more on that later in this chapter.

- *I will provide* one cartoon a day, every day, 365 days a year (366 on leap years).

- *I will always* be the author of the daily cartoon. I will not feature guest cartoonists to fill in for an absence.

- *I will not* use the daily cartoon as a promotion vehicle for $CORPORATION. What goes in the daily cartoon is limited to the story I wish to tell. Any products or services within the daily cartoon exist solely for the sake of the story.

- *I understand* that making a living from this is a privilege, not a right.

- *I will strive* only to run ads that are relevant to the audience.

- *I will not* gate off the cartoon to paying members only. I understand that not everyone has money to spend and that they can contribute in ways other than with cash.

- *I will always* remain within the boundaries of ethical behavior and will let my conscience be my guide.

In return, I hope:

- *You will respect* my intellectual property and acknowledge my sole right to determine how it will be used and distributed.

- *You understand* that content is not actually "free"; someone has to put their time, money, and/or effort into creating and distributing it.

- *You will support* me and the other independent creators whose work you enjoy through the purchase of memberships, visiting our advertisers, or even just by spreading the word and letting us know you like what we do.

- *You will not use* an ad blocker, particularly when you can turn the ads off by buying a membership.

- *You will not consume* content by Web-scraping or any other unsanctioned means that denies me or any other primary content creator pageviews and, therefore, ad impressions and, therefore, money to help keep their efforts afloat.

- *You understand* that you don't have a right to free content on the Net.

- *You will always remain* within the boundaries of ethical behavior and will let your conscience be your guide.

The optimistic tenor of this contract exists because I believe (and experience has borne out) that, for the most part, readers are well-disposed toward helping a favored content provider make a living. I should also point out that this contract is personal to me and what I do. For example, some cartoonists use guest artists and writers to cover their absences, and if they and their audience are okay with that, then who is to say it's wrong?

As an exercise, it would probably help you to draw up your own contract. If you like, start with mine and subtract what you don't agree with. Then add clauses that you feel are reasonable — or at least clauses to which you believe your audience will probably adhere. The assumption you should make while writing your contract is that your audience is of a reasonable nature. You'll never convince the ends (or at least one end) of the bell curve that your requests or expectations are rational. Don't waste your time trying — there are a lot of other things you could be doing instead of fretting over the actions of a small percentage of your readership.

Consumption Junction

Just before the twenty-first century, an Internet content provider even suggesting that he or she might monetize his or her audience to keep his or her site going would've been lynched, virtually speaking. There was an enormous ideological resistance to monetizing content that still exists today in a less pervasive form. Over the years, this resistance has faded largely, I believe, because of to the dot-com implosion. Many of the idealogues suddenly realized that it takes money to support a lot of Internet ventures, and that includes content provision.

There is still a very real resistance to advertising on the Internet, but the same can be said for all advertising and in all media. The key difference lies in the ability of the Internet consumer to take steps to block the ads, or at least consume the content without being subjected to ads. This difference exists because the consumer can control content that is on their computer.

When a user visits a Web page, all of the content of that page (graphics, text, and so on) are sent to the user's computer. The content sits on the user's hard drive and is normally viewed in a pre-determined manner through a Web browser. Most of the time, the user simply views the Web page as it is designed and delivered by the site owner. On occasion, there will be a user who sees the existence of content on his or her machine as the user's to manipulate as he or she pleases.

There is some merit in this position. If something is on your PC, you should be allowed to manipulate it as you see fit. Forcing Web browsers to display items in a particular way is, to some people, anathema and in their opinion against the spirit of free information. This position includes using ad-blocking software—and I'm referring to standard ad banner blocking, not pop-up or pop-under blocking—because the user doesn't like ads. To quote one user, "the ads annoy me."

The counter-argument states that (blue-sky ideals aside) reality forces the independent content provider to run ads. It is the one form of revenue-generation on the Web that is accessible to those with even the smallest audiences. The usual retort of "get a better business model" is glib and ultimately not useful. There are some small Realspace communities that have farmers who sell eggs by placing them in a box at the foot of their driveways, along with a sign that says "$2.00 per dozen," and relying on the honor system. No one tells the farmers to "get a better business model" because it's understood that it wouldn't be cost-effective for them to man a stall 24 (or even four) hours a day, but everyone wants fresh eggs.

As mentioned briefly before, an alternative to blocking the ads is a far more insidious practice: Web-scraping. This is where a user with Perl or PHP skills writes a script that visits a site and sucks down just those desired portions; in the case of my site, that would be the cartoon graphic. The script doesn't pull down any news or other text, avoids all of the other graphics, and most definitely skips the ads. Frequently, the user will aggregate material from several content providers onto one Web page that the user and his or her friends (or maybe even a wider audience) can view.

There is a real question of ethics here. Many of these people feel that it is acceptable to consume content on their terms, at their convenience, without giving anything back to the content provider. Their justification for this is often specious. They assert that "information should be free," twisting the concept (as discussed in Chapter 4) from the original "freedom to exchange research information" to the self-serving "all content should be free."

Some of the anti-ads audience also insists that, implicit contract or not, they didn't explicitly agree to it and, therefore, they in no way are bound by it. Of course, I disagree with their behavior (of continuing to consume content while blocking ads) if not the technicalities of their argument. The solution here is to interrupt a user's first visit to your site with a page that states the contract explicitly, and if the consumer agrees with it, they continue on. If not, they are given the opportunity to go elsewhere. This is kind of an End User License Agreement (EULA), although there is no force of law behind it.

As a rule, however, I'm not a big fan of impeding a user's journey through my Web site more than necessary. The more clicks it takes to get to your content, the more time the user has to decide it just isn't worth it and the user leaves for pastures perceived to be greener and freer. Until I see evidence that a significant percentage (say 10 percent or more) of my audience is being unethical, there is no reason to shove what amounts to an EULA in their faces. If it does come to pass, I'll confess I'll be irritated because 90 percent of the audience — the people who have been cool about supporting me — will have to deal with an annoyance caused by a very self-centered 10 percent.

Discontent over Content

There is an oddly socialist outlook on content prevailing on the Web in certain circles. Most of these audience fragments see content provision as a non-zero sum game; that is, they don't believe that it costs content providers anything to provide their work to the audience. Even in the case of a new blogger or someone who is uploading their artistic photos to Snapfish.com where there is no real costs involved in distribution (because they don't run their own Web site and pay hosting fees), there is a cost in time and effort. This concept is made a little clearer when spun around 180 degrees: *the content has value*, as determined by the audience.

Regardless of the direction with which you approach this point, content that you create has value invested in it. It's up to you as the creator to decide whether or not you want to give it away entirely, with no return to you other than admiration and gratitude. I'm an advocate of making a living (or at least some extra cash) as a content provider, and as such I'm also a big fan of the concept of TANSTAAFL, which was popularized by the science fiction writer Robert A. Heinlein in his novel *The Moon is a Harsh Mistress*. It stands for "Their Ain't No Such Thing As A Free Lunch," a colloquialism that posits you can't have something at absolutely no cost to you. This is the fundamental element of trade, where all parties exchange things of value, even if one of those things is a tangible and another is pure data. As long as each party feels they are receiving something of value, the trade is a fair one.

As difficult as it may be to believe, the ultimate reasonableness of this principle is lost on some people. At one point I didn't have any ads running on UF, and in fact funded it solely out of my back pocket. This was early enough in the cartoon's life that my audience was probably no greater than 100,000. I normally had five or six cartoons in the bank, ahead of schedule, but one day I ended up in the hospital and had to have surgery. I was hospitalized for about a week, and when I got home I realized that two days had gone by without any new cartoons — a friend had posted my medical status on the site for me to let people know I was still around but needed time to get caught up.

My mailbox was pretty full — the vast majority of the letters were from people who wished me good health and hoped I was doing better. One e-mail completely took me by surprise: a woman in West Virginia wrote a scathing letter to me, demanding to know where the cartoons were and how could I be so unkind as to ruin her week by being late? It's entirely possible she had a bad day, week, or even month, but, at the same time, consider what she's saying: that I owed her, that she was entitled to the content I produced at my cost.

I asked a UF audience member respected within the community for his clarity on ethics about this very point. This is what he had to say:

> "There are a lot of diverse situations in which the provider/consumer relationship exists online, and I think the answer to your question depends on which situation you're looking at. The ethics involved in producing news content for the Web, for instance, could require their own book. Once you've narrowed it down, however, I don't think the answer is very different from the answer to a parallel situation in the 'real world' — producing news content offline involves ethics that fill books as well.

> "To examine one scenario as an example: At UserFriendly.org, I engage in two different types of provider/consumer relationships. One of those is somewhat contractual. I pay a small monthly fee in exchange for being able to view the site without ads (also, of course, to support the site). The nature of the contract is technical — so long as I continue to pay the fee, the provider owes me an ad-free site; so long as I'm viewing the ad-free site, I owe the provider the fee. In such a contractual relationship, the provider ethically owes the consumer whatever the terms of the contract state he or she owes, and vice versa, just like they would offline. Rather simple, that.

"The other relationship is aesthetic, and that one is more complicated. The argument over what is owed by an aesthetic provider (I'll use the word 'artist') to their consumer is eternal. Does the artist make their work for themselves, or for their audience? For a classic modern 'real world' example of this, see George Lucas and the most recent three Star Wars films, which both George and a large part of his audience seem to agree were made for him first, and his audience second.

"Strictly speaking, the artist owes the audience nothing, because the audience can at any point stop the provider/consumer relationship by [in the case of free art] simply leaving or [in the case of purchased art] no longer buying that artist's work. If the artist decides one day to completely change the nature of their work, they risk losing some of their audience, but that is their choice. It is incumbent upon the artist to convince the audience to support them, but also within the artist's rights to not comply with the audience's wishes over their own. How to achieve that balance is, fittingly enough, an art.

"In terms of the audience owing the artist, I won't further pursue the loyalty aspect since I feel the last paragraph covered it. If they like the work, they'll support it; if they don't, they won't. There's not much more to say there. They are, however, ethically required to respect the copyright of the artist, which anyone who's been online in the last five years can tell you is something of a problem these days. People tend to think that 'online' = 'free,' even for purchased copyrighted works but especially for freely given ones such as Web comics or online articles. A Web site stays alive through its content, be it through the sale of said content or the ads surrounding it while it is viewed for free. A library in the real world allows you to view copyrighted works without charge, but not to copy them wholesale and distribute them to your friends. The same guidelines should exist with content on the Web — read the notice, it's almost always there. If it says you can look but not copy, that's what you can do."

— *"Ravenlock," Member of* UserFriendly.Org

The sentiments in Ravenlock's opinion are entirely logical from a functional perspective. If the content provider doesn't respect his audience's rights, he won't have much of an audience and will never be successful. If the audience doesn't respect the content provider's rights, the content provider will decide all the grief isn't worth it and pack up, which denies the audience access to his or her content.

Something also should be said about the comparison with other forms of advertising, such as television commercials. Consider this:

> "[A]dvertising performance is being gauged in a manner that fails to take into account the real effects of advertising. If I ask, 'what is the X-10?,' 95 percent of you are going to know what it is, even though probably only 33 percent of you have ever clicked on an X-10 ad. It's called branding, and on-line advertisers (for the most part) have failed to understand the importance of branding. This is funny because, before the Internet, branding was all there was. Think about it: You can't 'click-through' on your television, your radio, or your magazines. In those industries, advertisers are paying for potential. When someone plops down $1 million for an ad during some huge event, they aren't paying for guaranteed buys, click-throughs, or action. They're paying for the chance of getting a message to you. Meanwhile, you may be off in the bathroom, getting a beer, surfing channels, or hitting the mute button. On-line, there's an almost 1:1 ratio of ad views to ad income. It's measurable in real time. In every other industry, this isn't the case. Perhaps now you can see why Webmasters can get so infuriated at people who use ad blockers."

> — *Ken Fisher,* arstechnica.com

Where this leaves us as content providers is at a decision-point that we have to face every day. Look at your audience and your work. See how they are treating your expectations and always take a measure of how you are treating them. If there's an imbalance, you need to correct it. If you don't, or can't, you need to decide whether or not to pack it all up and go away. The hope is that you would never need to do this, that you can continue providing content on mutually agreeable terms. With the gatekeepers mostly out of the way, content provision has truly become a two-way street; for it to survive, both consumer and provider need to look both ways.

chapter

8

Protecting Your Creation

Nothing is more dangerous than an idea, when it's the only one we have.

— Emile Auguste Chartier, 1868-1951

In a near-perfect world, anything you create will be unmistakably yours. No one else would be able to rip off your ideas, or pass off your skill and talent as theirs. You'd be paid a reasonable amount every time someone enjoyed your content, and there'd be no go-between taking over half of the pie before you get your share.

In this near-perfect world, there would also be no taxes and no wars, and everyone would be dead sexy and joyfully traipse about in Lycra.

If you're one of that charming percentage of the population that believes in the inherent goodness of people, rest assured that you'll be disabused of that notion in short order should you create and publish anything that has even an inkling of appeal behind it. The depressing truth is that *people rip off other people*. Not to be outdone by the common man or woman, corporations, especially the big ones, rip off other people and companies with masterful efficiency. This is the reality of the business world today, and a source of constant concern for independent creators.

I'm also painting the world with too broad a brush. Clearly there are plenty of people who are genuinely decent, and companies who don't take their own measure solely from the bottom line. If neither existed, making a living as an independent creator would be nigh impossible.

The lesson here, then, is to always hope for the best but prepare yourself for the worst from other people and companies when it comes to how they treat your intellectual property. This means protecting yourself the best way you can, with full cognizance of the fact that you can't afford to have a battalion of IP lawyers hovering over your creations 24/7 with watchful eyes.

Protections *are* afforded to the common person such as you or me. Intellectual property law can be a stalwart friend to an independent creator, despite the vicious transformations it has undergone at the behest of the mega-corporations. And this is where I make my disclaimer:

I am not a lawyer. All of the commentary in this chapter is made from personal experience and my own understanding, which could be flawed or completely incorrect. My experiences are primarily with Canadian Intellectual Property law, but I've been made to understand that these are very similar to the law in the United States. When seeking to legally protect yourself and your creations, consult a legal professional, preferably an Intellectual Property lawyer. I have one myself and he is worth an order of magnitude more than the rate he charges. I also hope he doesn't read this book or my bank account is going to take a serious hit.

Now let's have a look at the tools at our disposal.

The Siblings: Copyright and Trademark

There are two related forms of Intellectual Property protection to discuss: copyright and trademark. They have a third sibling, the patent, but content providers generally don't deal with that one, because it pertains solely to the use, making, and selling of an invention. Patents are also the most complicated of the three types of intellectual property, complicated enough that patent law is an entire other specialty that exists outside of the practice of Intellectual Property law. Patents are also the most heavily legislated, expensive, and abused of the siblings. Be thankful that as a content provider it's very unlikely you'll ever have to deal with them.

(Technically, there's a fourth form of Intellectual Property as well, a kind of a third-cousin: the trade secret. This one I can safely sidestep because it pertains to processes and strategies that are deemed confidential within a corporate environment; if you do need advice on trade secrets, you'd probably want to read a book about them written by someone who has more experience with them than I.)

Copyright, Right?

There are a lot of misconceptions about what copyright really is. The most common one is that copyright protects ideas. This is incorrect, much to the chagrin of a lot of people who, struck with an idea they're sure will make them millions, find that their idea is, in fact, open season once they reveal it.

Simply put, copyright protects *the expression of information or ideas*, and not the information or ideas themselves. For example, you can't copyright a theme in a story, but you can copyright the expression of that theme. Philip K. Dick's remarkable story *Do Androids Dream of Electric Sheep* (which was taken to the big screen under the name *Bladerunner* starring Harrison Ford) uses the theme of Mankind asking questions we can't answer about our own existence. This theme has been used in countless other works, but Dick's expression of the theme in his popular story belongs to him. Thus, *Do Androids. . .* is copyrightable (and most certainly has been).

Anyone else can take the exact same theme from Dick's work and write another story based on it. The new writer can't simply lift the characters and world from Dick's work without expressed permission, but the new writer can write a knock-off that is reflective of Dick's writing. It's doubtful that the writer will be able to find a publisher that will pay for a clear knock-off, so it always better to come up with your own take on things. This is where talent reigns, where an artist who can express an idea with a fresh perspective will carve out his or her niche.

Copyright covers any original dramatic, literary, musical, or artistic work and grants you, as the owner of the copyright, the exclusive right to produce, reproduce, and publish that work or any part of that work in any material form. Generally, the person who creates a work (author, songwriter, cartoonist, and so on) owns the copyright. There is an exception. Employees who create a work for your company in the course of their duties (such as an employee manual) do not own the copyright; the company does. Also, contractors who are specifically producing creative works under a "work-for-hire" clause transfer all copyrights to you automatically. If you write a book and you want it translated, you must ensure that the contract has a "work-for-hire" clause in it, or the translator could end up owning the copyright to the translated work!

To qualify for copyright protection, there are two primary requirements you must meet:

- *The work must be expressed in a material form.* That is, it must be realized physically in some way. For example, the work must be written down on paper, or recorded as an MP3. I couldn't just teach the subject of this book to a class verbally; to claim copyright on it, I have to write down my ideas and information.

- *The work must be original.* This doesn't mean that it has to be original in the sense of being a brand new kind of story (it is widely held that there are only seven original stories, all cribbed from the ancient Greeks), but it must be the result of your efforts as the creator. As mentioned before, even mundane works such as employee handbooks can be copyrighted works.

A third requirement is more of a caveat. To pursue your rights in a nation that is not your country of residence, you must do so by way of the Intellectual Property laws that govern where you live.

One of the nicest things about copyright in North America is that you needn't take any sort of action to claim a copyright for something you've created. The act of creating a work automatically imposes copyright (as long as you meet the preceding requirements).

You can, if you wish, register your copyright for a given work. The Federal Copyright Office will give you an application package and charge you a fee for the privilege.

Registering copyright formally serves to create the legal presumption that you own the copyright in a given work, and the Copyright Office will send you a certificate to that effect. Keep in mind, however, that your claim to copyright will always (as in "forever") be open to challenge whether you are the true copyright owner or someone who registered the copyright, perhaps after copying someone else's work. If, for example, I don't immediately register a copyright for this book with the Copyright Office, and five years later I do so, I may find that someone has artfully claimed copyright for the work I have done. Of course, this would simply mean that I would have to challenge the copyright and have the offender thrown in a rat-infested dungeon. But you get the idea — registering copyright in a work doesn't necessarily grant you much benefit.

You may be wondering if what you do as a content provider even qualifies for copyright: podcaster, blogger who reports the news, or someone who provides content more as a process than as an art form. Rest assured that artistic merit is not the key here and is, in fact, irrelevant. For example, in the context of copyright, the term "literary work" doesn't refer to literature as in Charles Dickens' *David Copperfield*. As far as copyright is concerned, the book you're reading right now is a literary work; "literary" is, for the sake of copyright law, defined as expressions of ideas and information recorded in written form and can include source code, pamphlets, illustrations, poetry, screenplays, manuals, and courier waybills (!!). Copyright also covers "artistic work" (for photographs, blueprints, maps, sculptures, and so on) and "dramatic work" (for cinematography, recitations, mime, and so on). In short, if it's an original expression of an idea or information, and it is expressed materially, you can copyright it.

The list of things you can't copyright is considerably shorter in terms of definitions. As explained previously, you aren't permitted to copyright either information or ideas. The information in a multiplication table is not copyrightable, but your expression of the information in that table (designed with your own efforts) is.

You also aren't allowed to copyright common expressions of ideas and information. The phrase "Merry Christmas" can't be copyrighted, even if the mega-corporations like Disney or Coca-Cola would love to do so. We'll get into the abuse of Intellectual Property law a bit further in, but for now be assured that even the Big Evil Companies have a line they can't cross, at least thus far.

Lastly, single words, names, and titles are not protected by copyright. Rather, you have to apply for a trademark instead. I'll provide more on this later in the chapter.

In North America, copyright lasts for the life of the creator plus 50 years from the end of the year in which the creator passed on. If you created a work at any point in your life and you passed away in March of 2052, the copyright of that work would expire on December 31, 2102.

This brings us to the act of transferring copyright. As long as you are the true owner of the copyright, you may transfer it. To transfer the copyright in whole so that you no longer own any part of it, you must *assign* the copyright. If you just want to transfer an interest or right in your work, you *license* the work instead.

If you wish to assign your copyright, it must be done in writing and you (as the owner) must sign the paperwork. A lawyer's services are usually required for this.

There is one other aspect of copyright ownership that you should be aware of. As the creator, you have what is known as the "moral right" to the work, regardless of copyright ownership. If you assign the copyright of a song you wrote to someone, and they destroy what you consider to be the moral integrity of the song (say, by using a patriotic tune to denigrate your fellow citizens), you can stop them from using the song in this way. In other words, you remain in control of that work's integrity, and can stop anyone from detracting from the same. As the author, you can sue for damages and even demand that the assignment of copyright be returned to you.

The moral rights to a work cannot be transferred or assigned. At most, they can be waived, and to do so, the waiver must be explicit and in writing. An important part of the moral rights to a creation includes the right of the author to be associated with that work; copyright law protects an author's reputation with these moral rights.

Lastly, you should be aware of what constitutes *infringement* of copyright. Simply, it is the act of doing something with a work that only the owner of a work has the right to do, such as publishing it in whole or in part, where the person doing so is not the owner.

Taking a book such as this one and photocopying it is an infringement. Copying a movie on a DVD that you didn't produce is an infringement. Copying any work and then selling it is not only an infringement, it's a grievous one! The whole point behind copyright lies in a creator (and his or her licensees) deriving benefit from his or her hard work.

I've spent about a decade making mistakes as a content provider and learning from them, followed by several months of writing, editing, and researching to produce this book. My publisher is taking a financial risk with this work and spending money on editing, printing, and distribution. Therefore, it's only fair that the only two parties who derive any financial reward from the production and publication of this book are me and my publisher. If someone photocopies the book he or she is denying my publisher and myself the income we'd normally derive from a sale — and that someone stills gets to use the hard work and money that went into this book. If someone photocopies the book and sells the copies, not only am I not receiving any compensation, that someone is making money from my hard work! There are no dungeons deep enough for people and companies who rip off creators.

By the way — it's up to you to create a presumption of copyright in your work when showing it to others. Always clearly mark the work with a copyright notice that includes your name and the year of creation. For example, this book is Copyright © 2006 by Wiley Publishing, Inc., Indianapolis, Indiana.

Trademark, the Less (?) Popular Sibling

Trademarks are less popular than copyright in some ways: The common man and woman isn't too pleased with the idea that a rich company can trademark a word in the prevailing language and control some uses of that word. On the other side of the coin, companies love trademarks in that it gives them power over word sounds that may be in fairly common use. Overall, trademarks are arguably more contentious than the sibling, the humble copyright.

A trademark is defined as *a mark used to identify and distinguish your products or services from similar products or services offered by others*. The "mark" is most often a word or logo, but it can also be a series of initials (NASA), numbers (486), a slogan, a shape, or any combination thereof. Just about anything that can be visually recognized can be trademarked.

There is one principle requirement for something to be trademarked: it must be distinctive to the average citizen in your country (or any nation where your trademark is registered). This means you can't trademark something that closely resembles an already established trademark, such as shown in Figure 8-1.

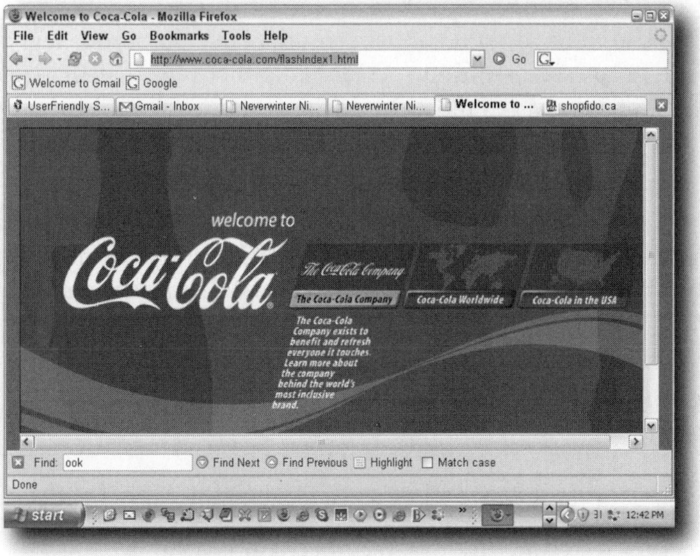

FIGURE 8-1: Some trademarks need no explanation

There are some things that you are not permitted to trademark:

- *Anything that is only descriptive* — As an example, you aren't permitted to trademark the phrase "Silk Stockings" because this would deny others the right to identify that their stockings are made of silk. However, you might be allowed to trademark a descriptive trademark if you waive all rights to the descriptive portion. So "Alpine Silk Stockings" might be a valid trademark as long as you disclaim any trademark rights in the words "silk stockings."

- *Anything deceptive or misdescriptive* — For example, you aren't permitted to trademark "Dominican Cane Sugar" if your cane sugar comes from Hawaii.

- *A person's name or surname* — This doesn't mean that you can't do business under your name (as many lawyers and accountants do, such as Dewey, Cheatum & Howe), but you can't hold a monopoly on the right to do so.

- *A trademark that may be confused with an already registered trademark* — A search is conducted at the Trademark Office to ensure that this is not the case.

- *Anything that serves only an ornamental purpose* — Your trademark must identify your goods and services, not just act as an ornament. For example, you can't trademark "Steel" but you can trademark "Steel Security."

Contrary to popular belief, trademarks do not need to be registered. Going to the Trademark Office and filling out the forms serves the same purpose as registering copyright — it's done to establish a legal presumption that your trademark is, in fact, yours, and is a valid one.

Establishing a trademark isn't difficult. Although you are not required to do so by law, it's a good idea for you to claim rights in your trademark by indicating it as such to the public. If your trademark hasn't been registered with the Trademark Office, place the letters ™ in the upper-right corner next to your trademark. If your trademark has been registered with the Trademark Office, you can use the symbol ® instead. With a registered trademark, you also have the option of using ™ instead.

Registration of your trademark does afford you some other benefits that aren't seen in copyright:

- You have the right to use the trademark in your country of residence.
- You can register the trademark in some foreign jurisdictions.
- You can prevent anyone else in your country of residence from using a trademark that is confusingly similar. In this case, it comes down to first-come, first-served.

A trademark lasts for as long as you use it to distinguish your products or services. If you register a trademark, the registration lasts for 15 years, unless renewed, expunged, or cancelled. A trademark registration is usually only expunged by a successful legal challenge — for example, someone who proves that they had been using a trademark much longer than you have.

Trademarks can be cancelled when they aren't used in connection with your products or services. To keep your trademark registered, you must ensure that it is being used, such as by ensuring it appears on your products when they are sold. If you provide a service, make sure that your trademark appears on your advertising and that it is conspicuous at the place where you perform your service.

Similar to copyright, you can transfer your trademark to someone else. Once again, you have a choice of *assignment* or *licensing*. If you assign the trademark, you're giving it all to the assignee. You can register the assignment, but not registering it doesn't make the assignment any less valid. If you license the trademark, you are giving the licensee the right to use the trademark. Make certain, however, that you retain full and direct control over the quality of goods or services that are sold in connection with your trademark. This is another case where a good Intellectual Property lawyer will save you expensive headaches down the road; find one to draw up a comprehensive licensing contract to protect your interests.

For example, as of this writing I have licensed the UF characters to a domain provider that I have personally endorsed. They use the characters in promotional art on their Web site, although we have agreed that I retain direct authority over the use of the art in promoting their services. The most recognizable character, Dust Puppy, is the *de facto* trademark for `UserFriendly.Org`, and, as such, he is the character most requested by my licensees, including the domain provider.

Infringement of trademarks has received a bit of press in the last few decades. Essentially, the rights of a trademark owner have been infringed when someone uses the trademark without someone's consent, although there are exceptions. The most notable one is to include a trademark in a book or other recorded medium for the sake of telling a story or illustrating an example. Provided the author of the book clearly acknowledges the trademarks as belonging to its rightful owner, the author is covered. Trademark owners mostly get annoyed when others use their trademarks to sell, advertise, or distribute goods or services — in other words, make money by unfairly using a trademark in which the rightful owner has invested a great deal of time, resources, and effort. This is a bit like copyright infringement, isn't it?

If you catch someone doing this with your trademark, you can sue for damages and have an injunction placed against them. A court can also order the destruction of any infringing goods that have the trademark on them.

Creative Commons — Ethical Protection

In this chapter, I've largely avoided discussing the egregious abuses that the large corporations (particularly media companies) inflict in the name of copyright and intellectual property. This is because what they do doesn't have a direct impact on what you as a content provider needs to be concerned with when you're just starting to get your business going. That doesn't mean that someplace down the road you won't want to be informed and concerned about their shenanigans in our places of government.

However, the contortions that make up a lot of Intellectual Property law today are well beyond the scope of this volume and really deserve their own book. There are, in fact, many on the market today and I urge you to go read some. Content providers on the Web need to stay informed about what our legislators are doing on behalf of moneyed interests, because many of the changes being made are good for them and detrimental to us, even as consumers.

A remarkable initiative was launched a few years ago on the Web known as the Creative Commons. The purpose of the Creative Commons is to offer artists and entrepreneurs protections that don't follow the "all or nothing" model of the traditional copyright. To quote them from their Web site:

"Creative Commons is a non-profit corporation founded on the notion that some people may not want to exercise all of the intellectual property rights the law affords them. We believe there is an unmet demand for an easy yet reliable way to tell the world 'Some rights reserved' or even 'No rights reserved.' Many people have long since concluded that all-out copyright doesn't help them gain the exposure and widespread distribution they want. Many entrepreneurs and artists have come to prefer relying on innovative business models rather than full-fledged copyright to secure a return on their creative investment. Still others get fulfillment from contributing to and participating in an intellectual commons. For whatever reasons, it is clear that many citizens of the Internet want to share their work — and the power to reuse, modify, and distribute their work — with others on generous terms. Creative Commons intends to help people express this preference for sharing by offering the world a set of licenses on our Web site, at no charge."

— From the Creative Commons FAQ at `http://www.creativecommons.org/`

(As per the requirements of the license attached to their FAQ section: You are free to copy, distribute, display, and perform the work — "the work" being the preceding quoted section — to make derivative works and to make commercial use of the work. However, you must always attribute the work.)

Figure 8-2 shows an example Creative Commons Deed.

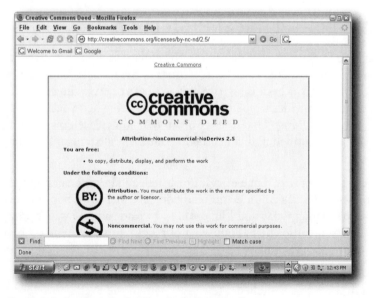

FIGURE 8-2: An example Creative Commons Deed

One of the greatest beauties of the Creative Commons is that it makes the language of copyright, licensing, and ownership of creative works accessible. As they so pithily point out, you can either examine the fully fledged legalese version of the contracts, or you can examine their "human-readable" versions. Also, as a content provider, you can use their site to "build" yourself a usage license according to your wants and desires. If you'd like to have your work shared as widely as possible and allow others to build on it, even if it means they can derive commercial benefit from doing so, you can create such a license. Or, you can protect yourself as fully as a standard copyright would allow. It is simply icing on the cake that the Creative Commons has a mandate to serve only the public interest, which happens to include both creator and consumer.

The Creative Commons is a collaboration by some of the brightest minds in cyberlaw today. Its chairman, Dr. Lawrence Lessig, is a professor of law at Stanford Law School and is an active advocate of giving the common man and woman better legal tools to work with than those afforded us by our own governments. His colleagues on the board are no less celebrated and I urge you to spend some time on the Creative Commons site, if for no other reason than to take advantage of the excellent legal resources there.

The Four Online Content Consumers

No discussion of copyright and ownership of digital content would be complete without delving a little into the psychology of the four major types of online content consumers:

- Thief
- Naïve
- Policeman
- Citizen

Many people exhibit behaviors that belong to more than one of the archetypes, but as a rule you're bound to find at least a few people who fall squarely into a single category. As content providers, it behooves us to be prepared for them because they can and do impact our financial success in what can be a pretty tough business.

Thief

The first of the major archetypes is the *Thief*—although this is a bit of a misnomer. (Copyright infringement, which is mostly what this person is actually doing, is a civil matter, not a criminal offense.) This person recognizes that this behavior is unethical, but doesn't care. In the mind of the Thief, all that matters is access to what he or she wants online, and he or she has no intention of paying for it, or compensating the content provider in any way. In short, if the Thief can have something for free and on his or her terms, the Thief will take it. If he or she can't, the Thief find a way to not pay for it, including cracking a site's security or stealing someone else's password. The Thief hates advertising of any sort and will block it, and won't care that this could spell the end of the content you create and distribute for free, because the Thief will just move on to another site. If you catch the Thief and call him or her on this behavior, the odds are the Thief will respond rudely and tell you that he or she didn't want your godawful content anyway. Overall, the Thief is not interested in helping the content provider, and is only concerned with personal wants and desires.

Generally speaking, the best way to deal with the Thief is to pursue him or her relentlessly—providing it makes financial sense to do so. I don't necessarily mean taking the Thief to court if you catch him or her, although that's certainly a possible avenue. Rather, I recommend you do things such as disable the Thief's account, ban the Thief's IP address from your site altogether, and perhaps even phone his or her mom. But don't waste so much time on the Thief that it's costing you productivity or sleep. You need to balance out the impact he or she is making by being a Thief and the impact your pursuit of him or her is having on your work. Be smart about it.

Naïve

The second major archetype is the *Naïve*. There are lots of these around, and they'd be entirely charming if it weren't for the fact that they can also be harmful to your living. These aren't necessarily unintelligent people, although they can lack perception. Their problem lies in their rationalizations: If content is digital, it's not "real," so it's not really stealing (which it isn't!—it's more accurate to call it "unauthorized distribution" or "copyright infringement"). Or, if they block the ads, it won't really hurt the creator, because the Naïve is only one person and how could one person doing this do any real harm? This archetype really exhibits more ignorance than malice, and if he or she were to know that these actions are directly harmful to the content provider, the Naïve would be mortified.

The best way to deal with Naïves is to educate. Many of them really do want to help their favorite content provider out but haven't thought through their actions entirely. This is where your connection to the audience can be so valuable. Engaging them in a dialogue about your rights and theirs can only help both parties.

Policeman

The third archetype is the *Policeman*. At first blush, the Policeman seems to be your ally, but time will reveal him or her to be an overzealous one. The Policeman is on the other end of the pendulum swing from the Thief. His or her plusses are a devotion to you receiving fair compensation for your work, which might include ad revenue and membership fees. The Policeman will be an advocate for buying memberships to your site, and patronizing your advertisers. The Policeman will also be ready to jump down the throat of anyone who even hints at doing something like blocking your ads, which to a struggling content provider might at first seem kind of nice. However, for every Thief the Policeman attacks, he or she will also flame three or four Naives. You can see how this could end up being destructive.

The Policeman means well, but his or her zealotry torpedoes the ability to discriminate between a Thief and a Naïve. Don't let the Policeman do this — insist that enforcement is your domain, and the domain of anyone you appoint as your agent. I do recommend that you put the Policeman to good use, such as by asking him or to report anything he or she spots as being shady.

Citizen

The last archetype is the most treasured one by online content providers: the *Citizen*. This is someone who understands that the content you provide costs and that creation and consumption only succeed in the long-term on a two-way street. The Citizen supports you by visiting your advertisers, or at least not blocking any ads on your site. He or she might buy memberships to access features and premium sections of your content offering. The Citizen exhibits the devotion of the Policeman, the well-meaning of the Naïve, and none of the traits of the Thief. In short, this is the perfect audience member.

This archetype is the one you want to cultivate. If you have a core of these in your audience, you will be well on your way to establishing a valuable, supportive audience. What more could a content provider want?

chapter

in this chapter

☑ What *Is* Fame Anyway?

☑ The Upside of Fame

☑ The Downside of Fame

☑ Pride, Praise, and Sycophancy

☑ How to Handle Criticism

Fame and Your Audience

Fame lost its appeal for me when I went into a public restroom and an autograph seeker handed me a pen and paper under the stall door.

— *Marlo Thomas*

At last! You have an audience of hundreds/thousands/millions. Very impressive, especially if you think that ten years ago the idea of having all of those people enjoy your work was a flight of fantasy. The Internet has truly helped open up communications between people in ways that we hadn't really considered before, and as content providers, we all get to enjoy the benefits of this new openness.

I included this chapter because I still get the occasional e-mail from start-up creators asking me how to deal with fame — quasi-, semi-, imagined, or otherwise. I certainly don't consider myself a celebrity (and with a backdrop of giants, I'm really just a small fish in a very large ocean), but I've given the entire fame situation a lot of thought. I did this because, like a lot of creators, I'm a bit of an introvert. As such, attention really isn't the number one thing on my list of "Most Desired." In fact, it's probably nowhere near anything of mine that even vaguely resembles a list.

Whether you enjoy attention or not, if you build an audience, you're going to be receiving it. Depending on how impactful your work is, this means you'll be getting letters of applause and gratitude, invitations to speak at conferences, questions from other aspiring content providers, and e-mail from people who really, *really* hate you and your work. This is all part and parcel of the fame game, and it's only smart to be prepared for what may be an incoming tidal wave.

What *Is* Fame Anyway?

Fame is the result of being known to the general public, or at least a not-insignificant portion of it. This is usually caused by doing something noteworthy, although some people are born into fame in a hereditary fashion. The British Royals are a good example.

Of greater interest is the fame that you, as a content provider, earn by doing what you do. You earn fame by saying, writing, drawing, making, or playing something that strikes some chord of resonance with the audience. Do it on a regular basis and your fame will grow. This is one of the tests of becoming a successful and widely watched content provider.

The moral opposite of fame is infamy, or notoriety. Either of them carries negative connotations. Some people who espouse extreme political views such as Ann Coulter and Michael Moore derive both fame and notoriety, depending on which side of the political spectrum you regard yourself. It's highly unlikely that you'll become famous without earning some notoriety, most notably among your detractors. And yes, you'll have detractors, even if they aren't particularly high-quality ones.

The Upside of Fame

Even for wallflowers (or introverts like myself), fame has an upside. Fame opens doors and greases the wheels of process. If you're famous enough, people offer you all kinds of perks, from free hosting to first-class airfare to wherever you're going, just so they can proudly say something like "*his (or her) site is hosted on our company server!*" People like to be associated with the famous, particularly those who they admire. Their admiration of you is what motivates them to extend a welcoming hand. Don't discount this, because it can greatly help you in your quest to earn a living.

An excellent example of the success that my fame (such as it is) has afforded me is this book that you are now reading. If it weren't for the fact that I have a large audience and some sway with them, it's doubtful that my publishers would've even considered selecting me to write about this subject. I have another example. At a hosting company UF once used, the techs e-mailed me to make it clear that if anything untoward happened to UF while it was hosted on their servers, they'd give it top priority simply because of who I was. I'm not a big fan of preferential treatment, but given that it was a Very Large Hosting Company and my requests could get stuck in the queue, I didn't object.

If you're someone who has a lot to say and you attract a sizeable audience, the time will come when you'll be invited to a conference or convention. Some of the time you'll be invited to just sit at a booth and hand out autographs. Occasionally, you'll be asked to sit on panels as an expert and discuss with other experts the questions of the day. At the top of the heap is an invitation to become one of the speakers (or even *the* speaker) at an event. This is where you get the chance to wax eloquently about the subjects that are dearest to you, all to a captive audience.

In all of these cases, you're invited mostly because the event organizers feel that you are famous enough to draw more attendees to their event. In some cases, the invitation is made with much consideration to a cost:effect ratio. If inviting Sharon the Famous Political Blogger costs us $1,000 to cover airfare, hotel, food, and taxis (and a speaker's fee in some cases), how many attendees would she need to help attract to make it worthwhile to our event?

This tends to make invitations that involve a lot of expense rare. It doesn't mean you won't get them, although they'll be fewer in number. I've had the very good fortune of being invited to dozens of places in North America thanks to what I do at UF, as well as parts of Europe, Australia, and Asia. Because I'm based on the West Coast of Canada, you can bet that the latter three regions have involved far fewer invites than the U.S.

By now, you will have come to the correct conclusion that fame is a kind of currency. You can trade it for other things, including money. Referring back to Chapter 5, "Branding and Merchandising," you'll remember the value of an endorsement. This is a way of trading your fame and reputation for someone else's dollars, and as such, needs to be done with exquisite care and consideration. If you don't, the chasm you'll slide down will be a deep one indeed.

It's important that you don't abuse the goodwill that you generate. A content provider whom I shall not name once did a truly despicable thing: he (gender neutral) used his goodwill to collect personal info about a large chunk of his audience and then sold it all to a marketing company. As a result, the audience members who trusted him and provided him with that information were spammed into oblivion! When I caught wind of this, I winced because it meant that some of my audience members who also used to enjoy the other guy's content would be understandably gun-shy about ever giving up their info again, and collecting marketing info in aggregate (not personally identifiable!) helps me generate revenue for my site.

So, where do you draw the line? I found this one of the easier questions to answer: *Don't ever assume that your fame will entitle you to anything.* If someone offers something, consider the ramifications and if it comes out positive take it. Otherwise, turn it down politely. There is no profit—monetary or otherwise—in being rude. A burnt bridge stays burnt.

The Downside of Fame

The only people I have met who have little or nothing to complain about being famous are "strong" extroverts. There even exists a subset of the extrovert crowd that actively covets and seeks out fame, with all of its blemishes and flaws. I can't say I'd ever understand their desire on an emotional level, but I do get it intellectually.

With fame comes many demands. At a public event, people will want your time. Your fans might crowd you or line up to get an autograph from you. There's only one of you and potentially thousands of them. How do you manage this?

Something to remember is that despite there being only one of you, every single one of your fans is an individual. Some will be star-struck, others will be down-to-earth, and yet others will act like they're your oldest friends (in front of all of the other fans, of course). Regardless of their behavior, it's critical that you remember they came to see you. People don't wait in queues for two hours to obtain your signature because they had nothing better to do. They do it because they value the content you provide them and want to obtain a sense of who you are in real life, even if only for a few seconds.

This demand can be an incredible weight on the shoulders of an introvert. After being in a crowd for a couple of hours I (like many other introverts) feel completely drained. Rather than looking for the shine of a spotlight, introverts prefer either the company of close friends and/or solitude. As someone who is famous and who has agreed to work a conference, however, your introversion matters naught.

Before I explain some of the duties that fame places upon you, let me clarify the point about crowds and introverts. Even as a fairly extreme introvert, I still enjoy meeting my audience in real life. It isn't really a weight as much as an obligation, and not an unpleasant one at that. I've had the benefit of meeting some fiercely intelligent fans who also happen to be some of the friendliest, most engaging people in the world. Having said that, I'd be lying if I didn't admit that even around such fine people, I become drained after a few hours. This is the result of my own personality, and no reflection on the people I've met. Mostly.

I have been made to understand that for the extroverts the constant attention from a crowd is energizing. This makes psychological sense because introverts derive their energy from solitude, while extroverts derive their charge from being around people. However, even extreme extroverts have admitted that, after a while, the whole crowd thing gets a little old. Departing and finding a much less focused spotlight is the usual remedy. If you're famous, you need to be prepared for this kind of experience. Bailing on an autograph line-up after an hour and brushing off dozens of people (or even just one person) who had waited all that time because you're drained isn't good manners. You need to recognize that fame is part of the content-provision game, and that fame has its costs.

One of the finest examples of dutiful celebrity is Peter Jurasik of (among many other productions) *Babylon 5* fame. I had the opportunity to meet him at a convention once, and stood in line to obtain an autograph. The line was more than two-and-a-half hours long, but I did eventually get to him. When it was my turn I walked up, shook his hand, and we began to talk.

This is where Jurasik really proved that he was a professional. Although he had already met and spoken to more than a hundred fans, he made me feel like I was the only person in the room with him. He spent only two or so minutes with me, but it felt like five or ten. He asked me engaging questions and offered a few bits of information about himself. He never, ever seemed rushed, and made sure that I got everything I wanted, including an autograph, a photo of him and me together, and answers to my questions. At the end of it, he thanked me for being a fan and never once made me feel like I was obliging him in any way. This kind of graciousness is what all celebrities should aspire to.

Jurasik also had a policy about autographs I feel is very sensible. A lot of celebrities today make their money by appearing at big conventions like Comic-Con and selling signatures. I've never liked that practice, because I feel any fan who has taken the time and borne the expense to come see me should be entitled to at least a few moments out of my day and a bit of ink on a book or shirt. Charging for an autograph strikes me as being awfully mercenary and a bit crass.

And yet, there's something to be said for charging for autographs. At another convention I had the delightful opportunity to sit next to Terry Pratchett at an autograph table along with a few other creators of varying fame. Pratchett was by far the heavyweight of the con, and his line stretched out the door. While I was taking a break between signings, I noticed a chap in Pratchett's line carrying an oily paper grocery bag. Most of the fans who wanted a Pratchett signature had brought their most treasured Pratchett book to be autographed, usually in hardcover. This one fellow dumped out his grocery bag in front of Pratchett and out spilled about 20 grungy, munged paperbacks of Pratchett's work. Pratchett didn't seem at all pleased, but he quietly and dutifully signed them all. In my opinion, the man has the patience of a saint. I'm quite sure I would've voiced my annoyance if I were in Pratchett's very famous shoes.

It was clear to me that the grocery bag guy wasn't a fan, but was some dullard who bought the books in a hurry at a used bookstore and had Pratchett sign them all so he could put them up on eBay. This is where Peter Jurasik's autograph strategy has considerable merit: Jurasik doesn't charge for the first autograph, period. Every other signature after is $20. The beauty of this system is that the real fans will always be able to get an autograph from one of their beloved celebrities at no additional cost. The mercenaries, the people who are there to make a buck off someone else's fame, will find it uneconomical to practice their trade. Everyone wins, except for the mercenaries, who are thwarted.

These two examples bring to light some of the complexities of celebrity. The complexities themselves are a downside, because you must consider what is fair and what the consequences are of any decisions you make in the way you interact with your fan base. Do you just go along with what your fans want out of you? Or, do you put restrictions in place, for the sake of your sanity? Where do you draw the line when it comes to making appearances? If you decide against attending public events, won't that harm your ability to make money? What if it doesn't?

Your duties as a celebrity can be summed up in a single sentence: *Give them as much of yourself as you can without doing harm to who you are.*

I recommend this approach because the members of your audience that seek you out generally want to get to know the brilliant mind behind the brilliant work, even if it means just getting a sense of who you are by your smile, handshake, or voice. There's also the whole bragging-rights thing that people covet when they meet someone famous. "Guess who I met the other day. . . ."

It makes good business sense to let your audience into your life a little. Being stand-offish in the Ivory Tower, as I've mentioned before, is a really bad idea. But that doesn't mean you need to invite everyone who says they're a fan into your home. Draw the line at "where you live" (not in the physical address sense, but in the "this is my life and really none of your business" sense).

There is one other thing you need to be aware of when you're famous, and it can be a real bugbear: people who want to ride on your coattails. Whether or not you're someone who enjoys fame, you can rest assured that you'll attract those who do, those who very much covet it for themselves. They'll hover over your shoulder and try to insinuate themselves into your work, in a grand hope to become at least as famous as you are—without committing one-tenth of the energy and effort you do.

Handling this sort of distraction can be simple (such as if you don't know the person) or complicated (such as if you're very close friends, or it's your boss). The former can be kept at a distance and safely ignored. The latter will involve some serious diplomacy on your part to disabuse them of the ludicrous notion that they deserve any portion of the reward for your hard work. Like some members of your audience, they'll feel you owe them, and they'll be hurt or deeply offended for not being included as one of "the special ones" (even if you don't treat anyone else as "special").

I have no catch-all solution for this problem, although I have found that ignoring the more obnoxious ones is a good general policy; they'll eventually go away, realizing their efforts are for naught. Also, be careful of allowing one or a select few access to your audience — if you allow for one, some others who feel they have a similar relationship with you will demand either their shot at the limelight, or an explanation as to why they've been excluded.

Pride, Praise, and Sycophancy

Long before they came into being in Europe, jesters were a fixture in the Imperial Chinese court. Unlike their European counterparts, however, the Chinese jesters weren't known to be mad or "fools." Rather, they were considered to be very wise men who had the ability to speak the truth in the form of a jest, thereby taking the sting out of criticisms directed at the King or Emperor, criticisms that were instrumental in helping the ruler realize any errors that were committed while the King or Emperor governed.

This "critiquing via jest" was also done by European "fools" who, rather than deemed wise and perceptive, were considered to be stark-raving mad. They were originally employed to lift a king or ruler out of melancholy, or assuage the ruler's anger through physical comedy, joke telling, and "acting the fool." The fool's potentially treasonous utterances as someone who was deemed touched with a child-like madness were excused as ravings, but satirical comments often made an impact on the ruler, and thus the jester served as an informal, but highly valued, royal advisor.

The history of the jester serves as an important lesson for people like us, people who aren't kings or powerful nobility. If we're to better ourselves as creators, we must ensure we don't surround ourselves with sycophants. It does the ego a lot of good to hear that you can do no wrong, but it also sets you up for a devastating fall when you first come across a detractor's comments about your work.

I've learned to temper my perception of my work over the years. If you're new at this game, or even if you've been at it for decades, you could fall victim to some pretty serious mood swings, and I'm not referring to the kind that come about from neurochemical imbalances. Most people need reassurance from their "tribe" as a form of social acceptance, and creators are no different. One day you could be on the top of the world after receiving one or a dozen letters of praise, and the next day you could be contemplating chucking the whole content provider thing and going back to slinging espresso at your local Starbucks because of some vitriolic, nasty letter that someone you've never met before wrote you. Or, you could hear absolutely nothing for weeks, and you'll begin to wonder if anyone's actually been reading your work. Finally, even without external influences taken into consideration, you'll begin doubting yourself. Rest assured that you aren't alone in this and that this kind of thinking is often par for the course. The trick is to not let it steer your decisions.

How to Handle Criticism

There's something to be said for having the cajones to put your work out onto the Web for all to see. You're in a vulnerable position, opening yourself up to smear attacks, nasty rejoinders, and criticisms from people who have nothing better to do. Communication on the Net is casual, and those who make negative remarks do so without thought because they suffer none of the usual social consequences for it. If you're an artist who has put your heart and soul into your work, and someone metaphorically uses it as toilet paper, you're going to be hurt.

And yet, so many creators are willing to weather the storm. Maybe it's because you've always wanted an audience, for better or worse. Perhaps you find strength in surviving baptisms of fire. Or, maybe you're trying to find out who you are by taking a measure of your emotional backbone. Whatever the reason, I take my hat off to you for at least trying. You clang when you walk, whatever your gender!

There is one very powerful tool to help you handle the kind of critic you'll most likely come across on the Net, and it was mentioned before: perspective. This is simply the most important thing to have ready while reading your fan (or hate) mail. It helps take the sting out of criticisms and mitigates the fanboy ravings with common sense. No matter how good or bad you are as a content provider, your work probably doesn't deserve any extreme levels of hype or the criticism aimed at you.

It helps to understand a couple of things about human psychology when it comes to subjectivity and social affirmation. When it comes to art of any form, people's tastes will vary. Pedro might get a kick out of your writing because he relates to it and shares some of your experiences, but Larry hates your work. Larry hates it because not only does he not share your frame of common experiences, he has his own framework that he feels is more valid and can't understand why anyone would enjoy what you write. And then there's Janine off in the corner, who is completely indifferent because her frame of reference is so unrelated to yours that her only comment about your work is "I don't get it."

Subjectivity also causes people to become defensive. If you enjoy a cartoon strip and someone else roundly criticizes it, that someone is not only attacking the value of the cartoonist's work, but also saying that you have bad taste. To the author, this squarely puts person A in the "he or she likes my work" camp and person B in the "he or she doesn't like my work" category. After a while, person B's comments just don't mean much. It's easy to tune out person B.

But what about people who used to be fans and are no longer? Does that mean your work is getting worse or that your talent has faded? Maybe all of those critics are right! Maybe the people who say "his work has gone downhill since X" have a point. They used to be fans, so maybe I am doing something wrong.

The odds are that you aren't and that your talent is still intact. It helps if you understand that everyone absorbs the same content in different ways, because we are each the sum of our experiences. A cartoon that is a laugh riot to some and merely amusing to others may fall flat for another group. Also, just because a given individual loves 30 percent of my cartoons but doesn't get or dislikes the rest doesn't mean that 70 percent of my work is tripe — it just means that for that person, 30 percent of my work resonated with that person, and the rest didn't.

It's ever so easy to draw spurious conclusions like this from the feedback you get. Some of the work you do will trigger the pleasure center for almost all of your audience. Some of it will only please another percentage part of the time. When you've been at the content game for a little while, even a matter of weeks, you'll learn that in no way is it possible to please everyone all of the time. The best you can do is to please yourself. As long as your work remains genuine and you stay on the course described by your own moral compass, you are doing all that any reasonable person can expect of you. Audience members come and go. As the author, you're the only constant with your work.

Having explored the problems of subjectivity, there will come a time when you'll find yourself tangling with people who, for whatever reason, have drawn conclusions that are *factually incorrect*. This isn't a serious problem while restricted to e-mail, but when someone posts an opinion about you or your work on a public forum that is based on spurious logic or false claims, you have some damage control to do. It doesn't really matter if the opinion is positive or negative — the truth, and your upholding of it, will always serve as the most ethical course of action. This is particularly important if someone posts falsehoods on your own forum, because your fan base will likely see them. Get in there and defend yourself; use supporting references and clear logic. For the most part your fan base will tend to side with you, and if you provide a clear, ethical stance, the lies of your detractors will reveal themselves to be what they really are.

This chapter wouldn't be complete without dipping into the psychology of rejection. You're going to face this a lot more than most people simply because you're putting your content out there for consumption. Dr. David Greenwald, a clinical psychologist (whom I quoted in Chapter 1) described a seminar he and his wife Wendy ran a few years back. Almost everyone who attended the seminar gave them high marks and thanked them for their help. One fellow, however, was the exception, and he said some unkind things about David and Wendy's presentation. On the flight home, did they think about the 99 people who said nothing but good things? Of course not. They couldn't get the negative remarks made by that one man out of their heads.

The current thinking in psychology circles regarding this suggests that this is a reptile-brain reaction. Remember that our reptile brains are only good at focusing on one thing: survival, which also includes security. Back when tribes were the dominant social group, criticism from even a single tribe member would cause one to fear for one's security and life. You couldn't afford to earn too many enemies within a tribe, or you may end up exiled. This usually spelled doom, because you would no longer have the security of numbers and you would be alone in your responsibility to gather food and find shelter. Your chances of finding a mate (and propagating your genes) would plummet. Overall, being criticized was a very real threat to face.

This fear has persisted through the ages, as it relates to our need to maintain acceptance and security within our social groups, even groups that are nothing more than audiences. It helps to understand where the fear is coming from, especially because it gives us perspective. Unlike the kings of old, we don't have the luxury of hiring our own jesters.

chapter

10

Ready, Fire, Aim!

Money is not the most important thing in the world. Love is. Fortunately, I love money.

—Anonymous

Congratulations! By now you should be armed with enough knowledge about the business of online content provision to get you started on the road to making some coin for your talents. But this book can only give you the tools and a bit of confidence from the knowledge you've absorbed; the perspiration and inspiration are solely yours to supply. That's the fun part.

Your next steps are fairly obvious. Aside from establishing your content, you'll need to do a few administrative things, including conducting a demographic survey, writing a privacy policy, deciding on a community behavior policy, and the like. I've provided you a checklist in this chapter to help get you organized.

Establishing your content means putting enough of it together to hook people to your creative talent. I recommend waiting until you have at least a few examples of work available (say, three or four podcasts, a dozen cartoon strips, a couple thousand words in a blog, and so on) before opening up for business. This presents an image to the visitor that you're at least a little committed to your work and that you're capable of doing more than just a one-off. I'm pretty sure most content providers would be happy not being labeled "The Knack" of the Internet. ("The Knack," for those too young to know them was the rock group who rose to brief stardom with their megahit song *My Sharona*. It was also their only hit ever, despite releasing a respectable six or seven albums. And yet, they're often considered the epitome of the one-hit-wonder.)

The Content Provider's Business Checklist

Following is a list of things you need to take care of:

- Establish content
- Write a privacy policy
- Write a forum policy for acceptable use
- Write copyright terms
- Sign up with an ad network
- Crank up the marketing
- Collect demographic information
- Build a media kit
- Contact a third-party ad sales force or more ad networks

Establish Content

You already know how to do this better than anyone else, because it's your content you're creating and establishing. Just remember to have enough there to get people hooked and wanting more.

Write a Privacy Policy

You can use the one I use for UserFriendly.Org if you like (see Figure 10-1). Alternatively, you can cobble together one of your own by borrowing from other privacy policies (just don't copy them whole without permission). Remember that the goal of a privacy policy is to let your audience know what you intend to allow to happen to their information. I do caution you that most audiences won't be too appreciative of a privacy policy that gives the site owner the option to sell their personal information to, say, a telemarketing firm.

Also note that it helps if you post clear links to the privacy policies of corporate sponsors and your regular advertisers. This way, your audience is made aware of how their information will be treated on the sites they visit through one of your links. There's no need to do this for advertisers who run bulk Run of Network ads on your site. This is more of a courtesy than a necessity.

We respect your privacy! Any and all information collected at this site will be kept strictly confidential and will not be sold, reused, rented, loaned or otherwise disclosed. Any information you give to us will be held with the utmost care, and will not be used in ways that you have not consented to.

[**your site name**] does not sell, rent, loan, trade, or lease any personal information collected at our site, including survey forms or email lists.

[**your site name**] occasionally analyzes our website logs to constantly improve the value of the content available on our website. Our website logs are not personally identifiable, and we make no attempt to link them with the individuals that actually browse the site.

[**your site name**] launched a voluntary registration system for users in [**date**]. Individuals must affirmatively request to join our mailing lists by signing up through a form on our web site. We will not sell, rent, loan, trade or lease these addresses on our list to anyone, though we will use this mailing list to keep members informed of upcoming events and to market our services and products.

If you have any additional questions, please contact us at [**email address**].

FIGURE 10-1: Example privacy policy

Write a Forum Policy for Acceptable Use

Once again I've provided one you can use from `UserFriendly.Org`, included in Figure 10-2. The point behind this policy is to help govern the interactions among your audience members in your forums. If it doesn't matter to you if people swear in your forums, you can take the rule against swearing out. It's a mix-and-match really and like all other policies is the purview of the site owner.

Write Copyright Terms

This is where the really great folks over at Creative Commons (`http://www.creativecommons.org/`) come in handy. Their "Copyright License Builder" helps you construct a copyright deed that you can post on your site, in both the full legalese version and in what they call "human-readable form." You can find the builder at `http://creativecommons.org/license/`.

- **The First Rule**
If your post would blatantly contribute to diminishing another member's enjoyment of the forum, don't post it. This rule is the basis of the other rules.

- **The Second Rule**
No personal attacks or insults are allowed. This rule mandates that you only attack someone's line of reasoning, if anything.

- **The Third Rule (also known as the FYOSR)**
Post nothing that you wouldn't want your Fourteen Year Old Sister to read. Another way to look at this rule is to ask yourself if you'd want your boss, mother, uncle or someone else you respect to read what you wrote. If the answer is "no," don't post it. A rational discussion about sex is fine. If the language is inappropriate for an average newspaper, or if it's something you wouldn't hear a CNN anchor say, it is most likely not welcome here.

- **The Fourth Rule**
Post nothing illegal. Links to warez sites, pirated media or child pornography will cause the site owner to pick up the phone and call the authorities. Understand that the owner of this site *will* cooperate with law enforcement to the fullest extent to have your criminal backside thrown into prison.

- **The Fifth Rule**
Don't be guilty of an "-ism." This means racism, sexism or their siblings. If you post something about "n*ggers" being lynched, you had better be offering some kind of historical perspective. Hate literature and the advocacy of violence against other human beings are not permitted in this forum.

- **The Sixth Rule (also known as the 2-Click Rule)**
You may not link to any pages that break any of the previous rules, especially the FYOSR, within 2 clicks. This means that a link, any link, you provide is the first click and all links on that page are the second click. Any page that breaks this rule will get you moderated, at the very least.

FIGURE 10-2: Example forum policy

Figure 10-3 shows what I use myself for UF's copyright needs.

If you're going to be running a public or private forum, you'll also need to decide who owns the comments posted by your audience. Some site owners feel that the comments should become site property as soon as they're posted, whereas others maintain that the comments remain the property of the poster. The former approach precludes you having to ask for user permission should you ever wish to use any of their writing for promotional purposes or for research. I'm more of a fan of the latter approach, because it absolves you as the site owner for any remarks made by a user that could land you in legal hot water. At most, your responsibility will stop at being compelled to remove illegal posts from your site.

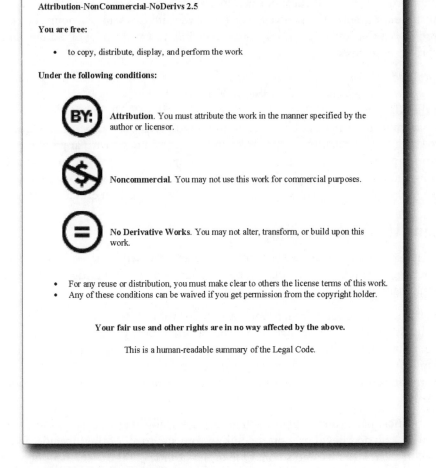

Attribution-NonCommercial-NoDerivs 2.5

You are free:

- to copy, distribute, display, and perform the work

Under the following conditions:

Attribution. You must attribute the work in the manner specified by the author or licensor.

Noncommercial. You may not use this work for commercial purposes.

No Derivative Works. You may not alter, transform, or build upon this work.

- For any reuse or distribution, you must make clear to others the license terms of this work.
- Any of these conditions can be waived if you get permission from the copyright holder.

Your fair use and other rights are in no way affected by the above.

This is a human-readable summary of the Legal Code.

FIGURE 10-3: Copyright example

Sign Up with an Ad Network

So, now you have your legalese in place, your content established, and your Web site is rolling. People have started visiting your site (your friends and family to start with, of course) and word is beginning to spread. Now's the time to get a bit of passive income going.

Passive income is the best kind — it means you're earning dollars all of the time without your direct influence. Normal income is active in the sense that you trade your time for money. With advertising on a Web site that runs 24 hours a day, seven days a week, you're earning coin even while you're sleeping or reading your favorite comic book.

A great ad network to start with is with Google's very popular AdSense (`https://www.google.com/adsense/`). AdSense gives you the option to select color schemes for the ads and it provides a variety of ad sizes. I still use AdSense to backfill any unsold inventory I have at UF. Keep in mind, however, that AdSense is a Cost-Per-Click (CPC) deal. If no one clicks on the ads, you don't earn anything. I still recommend AdSense for beginners because Google doesn't insist that you have a minimum number of pageviews per month before they'll approve your application. Also, you can bail on them at any time — they don't expect an exclusive from you.

Crank Up the Marketing

You have content, people who consume it, and an ad network (hopefully) generating money for you and through your Web site. Your next step is a critical one — crank up the marketing!

If you're serious about creating more income for yourself from your content, you absolutely, positively must always be thinking about how to obtain a larger audience. Given the medium, this might mean something as simple as a "Tell Your Friends About Us!" notice on your home page to something as complex as a system that rewards your audience members for referrals that create more account sign-ups.

For the most part, your audience will grow organically. If your core members really like what you do, they'll pass on the link to your site to all of their friends, and they'll tell *their* friends, and so on. One of the beauties of the Net lies in how easy it is to share things that you like with your social circle. A quick e-mail with a copied and pasted URL takes seconds, and can go out to hundreds of people with the click of a button. The UF site even has an "Email This Cartoon" button over every cartoon strip in the archives so that readers don't even need to open their mail client to send out the URL to their friends.

Despite this organic growth you can expect, you shouldn't ever assume that "things will take care of themselves." At the beginning, when your content is particularly fresh and new to the world, it behooves you to continually promote your site and material. I don't recommend you be obnoxious about it, but don't be complacent either.

Take advantage of hub sites that attract a lot of attention. Some good ones are Podcast Alley (`http://www.podcastalley.com/`), Technorati (`http://www.technorati.com/`), and Keenspot (`http://www.keenspot.com/`). List your site wherever you can, including on the search engines, but do it without being obnoxious (such as by spamming several UseNet newsgroups). The idea is to get the word out as widely as possible, to get people visiting and talking about your work. The more people that show up, the more likely it is that more people in the future will show up as well, and when you have a large amount of traffic, you'll have more ad inventory from which to generate revenue.

Above all, remember that sitting back and expecting your site's natural growth (whatever the rate might be) to be enough is tantamount to inviting stagnation. Just because you've built it and they're coming in droves doesn't mean you should sit on your laurels! If you want to make a splash, keep pushing! *Hope is not a strategy!*

Collect Demographic Information

So, now you have all of that going on, where to next? Remember Chapter 2, "The Advertising Game"? Demographics are the key here, and when your audience is in the thousands, it's time to start finding out who they are.

If you were forward-looking and built in a survey for new accounts, good for you, you're on your way to understanding who your audience is. If not, no problem — you'll need to run a survey and collect the data. This information will not only help you get a picture of who consumes your work, but it'll arm you with data that can help you make more dollars.

Since you've read all the way through this book, I'm sure that after you get all of that demographic data, you know what to do next.

Build a Media Kit

You can either build one for the Web only (pure CSS and HTML, perhaps Flash) or you can build one for print with, for example, Adobe Acrobat. Whichever way you go, copy someone who's already done it to good effect. A Google search for "media kit" reveals dozens of excellent examples. The *USA Today* media kit, built with Flash, is one from which you can easily borrow a dozen ideas! If you'd rather have someone else do your media kit for you, there is no shortage of creative houses that specialize in this kind of thing, although most of them do require that you come up with some cash. Either way, remember that you must be armed with a media kit before you approach a third-party ad sales force; I guarantee it'll be one of the first things they'll ask for.

Contact a Third-Party Ad Sales Force or More Ad Networks

Now you need to find a professional sales force that is willing to represent you in the media selling game. Most sales forces won't be interested in bringing you aboard unless you can promise them a sizeable ad inventory, say in excess of 5 million ad impressions a month. If you have less than this, and still want to ramp up your income, consider joining more ad networks and give weighted portions of your inventory to each one. There are also some boutique ad networks out there that specialize in niche markets. These tend to bring in higher CPMs for access to particular audiences, such as IT-heavy ones, or audience groups that play a lot of computer games.

Part-Time Fun to Full-Time Living

I've been rich and I've been poor. It's better to be rich.

— Gertrude Stein

At some point during your foray through this book, you might have changed your goals about your shot at the content-provision game. If you came into this book with a wish to learn how to make a bit of beer money, you might have come away with the burning desire to make it your full-time living. Or perhaps you had that in mind to begin with, but faced with some of the realities of the things that need doing in a business endeavor you've adjusted your sights to start a little smaller. Either way, everything you've learned in this book can be put to good use.

The harsh realities of money-making and spending behooves every one of us independent creators to get a good handle on what we're risking on a monthly basis. The good news is that, for the most part, our overhead costs when we're starting out tend to be minimal or even zero! Bloggers simply need to start up a blog at `blogger.com`, for example, at no cost to them at all. Podcasters do need their own Web site (and a dedicated domain is always a good idea) that allows for large downloads, but hosting that fulfills this can be had for less than $10 a month. Cartoonists can begin their foray on the Web with a free account over at `Keenspace.com`, but once they generate a sizeable audience, they would be better served to rent their own Web space, again for a minimal amount. This is one of the most beautiful things about content provision on the Web: the hard costs can be so low as to be insignificant, so while you're exploring your art, you do not have to get a second mortgage on the house.

Things can get expensive a bit farther down the road. As of this writing, User Friendly.Org does around half a terabyte of traffic a month, and we're down to that thanks largely because of some optimization code. (At one point we were pushing a full terabyte!) However, advertising revenues and paid memberships take care of the hosting costs and still leave enough left over for me to pay for the roof over my head and the baked beans and Ramen I have come to learn how to serve in millions of ways. And after that, there's still enough left over for me to pay my business manager and a few contractors I use from time to time. Thus, the traffic I get costs me more but also creates an opportunity for me to generate more revenue.

Note in the last sentence: *creates an opportunity for me to generate more revenue.* This means that, as my traffic increases, I have to take the responsibility to ensure that I'm making more money from it. Don't assume that your ad networks will pick up the slack for you, even though they may very well do so. In business, it serves no useful purpose to assume that someone else will take care of your interests for you. In fact, thinking that way is a surefire recipe for financial suicide. It's your content, your site, and your interests — be sure to shepherd them attentively.

Final Words

It's ever so important as you start on your journey as a professional content provider that you keep your goals and milestones clear in your mind. Do you want this to become a full-time job? Do you want an exclusive country-club sort of site where all of your audience members pay to get in? What kind of audience are you aiming to attract? What are you getting out of this as an artist, besides money? By next year, how many people do you want reading your blog? How far around the world do you want your podcasts to be heard? All of these questions and more are only yours to ask and answer. Review your goals at least once a week, and adjust them when your gut tells you to. Until then, stand by them and work toward their (and your) fulfillment.

I hope that what I have been able to teach you makes a positive impact in your life and helps you reach the goals you have set for yourself. Money aside, making content for others to enjoy is its own reward. What creator hasn't thrilled at the reaction of an appreciative audience? What writer hasn't felt vindicated when others cheered the hero of the story? Or name a cartoonist who, seeing a child giggle at a rendering of a favorite character, hasn't smiled and felt that it was all worth it just then? The time we live in, with the birth of the most powerful communication medium in history, is ripe with opportunity for people like you who have stories to tell, opinions to air, images to share, and satire to stage. You also have the opportunity to do something you love every day of your life and be paid for it.

This brings me to the end of this book. Appended to this chapter you'll find a few useful reference pages and a bibliography that includes some books I highly recommend you take the time to read if you'd like to broaden and deepen your understanding of online content. I'd love to hear from you if you have a creator's success story to tell, no matter how minor, or if you'd like to see something added to future editions of this book. Visit `moneyforcontent.com` and drop me a line, and, if you're so inclined, join the forum there to share your story with your fellow content providers.

Thank you for reading! It is with sincerity that I wish you the best of luck and all success in your endeavors as a creator.

References and Resources

This appendix provides important reference information in the following areas:

➤ Online advertising resources

➤ Advertising networks

➤ Blogging resources

➤ Podcasting resources

➤ Copyright and other legal resources

➤ Ethics resources

➤ Online community tools

➤ Bibliography

Online Advertising Resources

Following are some key advertising resources:

➤ *Interactive Advertising Bureau* (`http://www.iab.net/`) — An association that focuses on assisting, guiding, and setting standards for online content companies to increase their revenues. Much of the standardization of Web advertising is done by this group.

➤ *ClickZ's Ad Resource* (`http://www.clickz.com/resources/adres/`) — Packed with links to articles and other resources on online advertising and marketing. Roughly half of the links are useful; I found the other half to be chaff, but your mileage may vary.

➤ *iMedia Connection* (`http://www.imediaconnection.com/`) — Dense with information on the art of online marketing and advertising. The site has some useful reference sections, such as one listing a dozen of the bigger ad networks.

Advertising Networks

Following are some key advertising network resources:

- *Google AdSense* (`https://www.google.com/adsense/?sourceid=ASO&subid=US-HA-06Jan05`) — Not an actual network per se because they stick to a single formula, but that formula does work. AdSense makes Google a staggering amount of money which seems to increase every year. Remember that this is a CPC (Cost Per Click) model, so there is no guaranteed revenue for running the ads on your site. Still recommended, especially for the just-starting content provider.

- *Tribal Fusion* (`http://www.tribalfusion.com/`) — One of many ad networks out there, but I've personally found their payments to be timely which is important, and they're a bit of a boutique outfit. They're easy to work with as well. You'll need to have demographic info and at least a half million banner impressions available before you approach them though.

- *24/7 Canada* (`http://www.247canada.com/`) — Much like Tribal Fusion and other ad networks, but this one specializes in Canadian markets. If you have a sizeable Canadian audience, these are the guys you'll want to talk to. Demographics data is once again important.

- *24/7 Real Media* (`http://www.247realmedia.com/`) — The U.S. mothership of 24/7 Canada; one of the really huge ad networks. Don't expect to get much attention from them unless you have serious (more than 10 million) inventory and dead sexy demographics. If not, they still may sign you up, but you'll be lumped in as one of many scores of smaller sites and given RON (Run Of Network) ad campaigns; generally non-targeted with low CPMs and CPCs.

Blogging Resources

Following are some key blogging resources:

- *Technorati* (`http://www.technorati.com/`) — This very spiffy site keeps track of what is going on in the world of Blogs, amalgamating blog data and reporting on which bloggers are rising in importance, what ideas are coming out of blogspace, and how fast the information is being passed around. If you blog, you need to sign up with these guys.

- *ProBlogger* (http://www.problogger.net/) — If you'd like to pick up some valuable tips on making money as a blogger, this is a good site to explore. It doesn't tell you the whole story (nor does it pretend to), but it's a good springboard for the blogging niche.

Podcasting Resources

Following are some key podcasting resources:

- *Making Podcasting Audible* (http://www.audible.com/ podcastingprofit/) — Audible.com has owned the audio books space on the Net since they began years ago. Now they're offering podcasters a chance to use Audible's own marketing and management expertise to make some coin. They'll be your business partners, as it were. No doubt there is an opportunity here, but as with all things, be careful of what you agree to.

- *Podcasts.com* (http://www.podcasts.com/) — As expected, this is all about podcasts. They offer a huge assortment of programming to choose from, but most important of all, they're in the business of helping podcasters make money. They can be very specific about what they're looking for in podcasts, and, in exchange for their help, they take a cut of the money pie.

Copyright and Other Legal Resources

Following are some key copyright and other legal resources:

- *Creative Commons* (http://creativecommons.org/) — One of the most important sites covering the question of digital copyright in our day and age. Go here and make yourself a Rights Deed! All of the information is free, and supplied by experts. Dr. Lawrence Lessig himself (among dozens of other luminaries) is involved.

- *Copyright Law of the U.S.A.* (http://www.copyright.gov/title17/ 92chap1.html) — A U.S. Government Web site that details U.S. Copyright Law in its entirety. Dry reading of course, but crucial if you'd like to understand what copyright really is.

Ethics Resources

Following is a key ethics resource:

- *Dr. Lawrence Lessig's Blog* (`http://www.lessig.org/`) — Dr. Lessig is a Professor of Law at the Stanford Law School and is well known for his thoughtful ideas and arguments regarding copyright and intellectual property. Above all, he seems most concerned with the greater good and encouraging advancement and innovation. For these reasons (and several others), I recommend that you stop by his site every now and then just to catch up on what he's been pondering.

Online Community Tools

Following are some key online community tools resources:

- *PHPBB* (`http://www.phpbb.com/`) — Free Online Forum software, perhaps the most popular package of its kind on the Web today.

- *Online Community Toolkit* (`http://www.fullcirc.com/community/communitymanual.htm`) — This simple Web page is a collection of links to articles, tools, and other resources that can help steer you in the right direction if you're looking to getting your own online community up and running. This is updated sporadically.

- *Groupee* (`http://www.groupee.com/`) — Feature-rich forum software predicated on the service module. You pay from $15 a month to have their forum software run where you want it, the way you want it, and they handle the technical side entirely. A lot of customization is available.

- *PostNuke* (`http://www.postnuke.com/`) — Extremely popular, free Content Management Software (CMS) that includes an extensive forum module. Highly customizable. Not extremely secure but better than some other packages.

- *Drupal* (`http://www.drupal.org/`) — Powerful and secure CMS with solid forum module. As customizable as PostNuke, but requires somewhat more technical knowledge to install and run.

- *CMS Wiki* (`http://www.cmswiki.com/tiki-index.php`) — Extensive knowledge base of Content Management Systems, including reviews of software packages and developments in the CMS world. Can be quite technical.

Bibliography

Caples, John. *Tested Advertising Methods*. Paramus: Prentice-Hall, 1998.

Gardener, Susannah. *Buzz Marketing with Blogs For Dummies*. Hoboken: Wiley Publishing, 2005.

Holt, Douglas B. *How Brands Become Icons*. Boston: Harvard Business School Publishing Corporation, 2004.

Klein, Naomi. *No Logo*. Toronto: Random House of Canada, 2000.

Lessig, Lawrence. *Free Culture*. New York: The Penguin Press, 2004.

Levinson, Jay C. and Lautenslager, Al. *Guerilla Marketing in 30 Days*, Irvine: Entrepreneur Press, 2005.

Nordling, Lee. *Your Career in the Comics*. Kansas City: Andrews and McMeel, 1995.

Surmanek, Jim. *Advertising Media A to Z*. New York: McGraw-Hill, 2003.

Surman, Mark and Wershler-Henry, Darren. *Commonspace*. Toronto: Prentice-Hall Canada, 2002.

Index

Continued

Continued

Continued

How to take it to the Extreme.

If you enjoyed this book, there are many others like it for you. From *Podcasting* to *Hacking Firefox*, ExtremeTech books can fulfill your urge to hack, tweak and modify, providing the tech tips and tricks readers need to get the most out of their hi-tech lives.